VICTORY in the WILDERNESS

VICTORY in the WILDERNESS

Understanding
God's Season of
Preparation

JOHN BEVERE

Victory in the Wilderness:
Understanding God's Season of Preparation
by John P. Bevere

Copyright © 1992 by John P. Bevere

ISBN 0-9633176-0-1
Printed in the United States of America

Library of Congress Catalog Card Number: 92-090341

Published by Messenger Press
an extension of John Bevere Ministries, Inc.
P.O. Box 2002
Apopka, Florida 32704-2002

Direct inquiries and/or orders to the above address.

Cover art by Doug Belew/Belew Design, Tulsa, Oklahoma
Cover photo by Dennis Rosenquist, Orlando, Florida

ACKNOWLEDGMENTS

My deepest appreciation to . . .

all those who labored with us in prayer, in project, and by financial support to bring this book to completion; to Steve and Sam for their constant encouragement and technical support; to Scott for his wise counsel and Amy and Annette for their many talents.

I want to thank my wife, Lisa, who continually encouraged me and selflessly helped with editing, but more important, for the godly wife she has been to me. A special thanks to my three sons who sacrificed time with Daddy that this project could be completed.

Most important, my gratitude to my Lord Jesus for His grace and companionship during this project and the Holy Spirit's faithful guidance throughout this work.

CONTENTS

FOREWORD

John Bevere has a prophetic message for today, a message from God, a message that is backed up by the full counsel of God's Word. After spending seven years in the "wilderness" seeking God and studying His Word, I wondered in this day of prosperity teaching and "I've got to be happy at any cost" philosophy if anyone would accept the word God had been teaching me. Then I received John Bevere's book, *Victory in the Wilderness*. As I began to read it in my prison cell, my heart leapt, for here was the same message the Holy Spirit had been breathing to me. John cries out that it is time we seek the Lord for who He is, not just for the promises, but for the "Promisor" Himself.

Shortly after I read *Victory in the Wilderness* I received John Bevere's next book, *The Voice of One Crying*. After reading this prophetic book, I felt I just had to meet this John Bevere. I had to see if he was for real. Could God have given this urgent, eternal, last-day preparation message to this young preacher? Knowing of John's theological background, I just had to

know if he really believed what he had written. (I have inter-
viewed thousands of authors and many didn't know and
others didn't believe what they had written about . . . they
were just good at the craft of writing.) I asked for him to come
to see me in prison and he did. When John walked into my
prison, I knew this was a man sent by God, a modern-day
"voice of one crying." I wept as we shared together; John
Bevere was for real.

Victory in the Wilderness and *The Voice of One Crying* are
two of the most important books of this hour; they hold the
keys to the Church's survival. I have had these books sent
to hundreds of my friends and to key leaders. They are
"must" reading for those who want to serve and obey
Christ and be a part of the last-day harvest time of souls.
You may wonder why many Christians and church leaders
today are in the pigpens of life like the Prodigal Son. The
Prodigal Son said to his father, "Give me," and ended up in
a far country, in the wilderness, in a pigpen. John Bevere
teaches us how to get back to the Father's House.

—Jim Bakker

INTRODUCTION

This is a book about the wilderness—a place or time period through which every Christian must pass as he draws nearer to God. It is not a time for seeking signs or wonders, but a time to seek the heart of God, which will produce character and strength in the believer. It is a preparation time—a time that may appear discouraging without the vision of the promise. It is my hope that this book will bring encouragement as you sojourn in your pursuit of Him Who alone satisfies.

I do not claim that this is an exhaustive or all-inclusive study; there is much more that can be written, but this account is from my heart. The intent of this book is to introduce this subject to you, then allow the Holy Spirit room to apply it to you personally. I purposely have stayed away from giving detailed examples from my life, to avoid influencing your application of this message to your own life. Everyone's wilderness will consist of different circumstances.

Upon my arrival in the wildernesses, I met confusion, frustration, fear, suspicion, loneliness, discouragement, and anger. What was I doing here? This was not my destination! Yet, I had cried out to God to rend my heart, purify my motives, cleanse me of all secret hidden sin, refine my vessel, and remove any hindrance to His glory. But I did not expect the process by which He chose to accomplish this in my life. This book is my journey to the wilderness, as well as that of many others. I have not "arrived," nor have I attained all that God would have for me, but it is my prayer that in these pages you will find the strength and courage to press on toward your destiny in God.

If there is an understanding of your position in life, it brings your life into perspective. Then you can see God's hand, even when you may not feel His touch. It is a time when your love for Him matures beyond "What will He do to benefit me?" and turns to "What does He desire of me?"

SECTION 1

THE WILDERNESS

CHAPTER 1

THE WILDERNESS SEASON

In frustration, you remember the times when you merely whispered His name and His presence immediately manifested, but now in the stillness you want to shout, "God where are you?"

Look I go forward, but He is not there and backward, but I cannot perceive Him; when He works on the left hand, I cannot behold Him; when He turns to the right hand, I cannot see Him.   Job 23:8-9 (NKJV)

Is this your heart's cry? You long to hear from God but all you sense is silence. You pray—yet your prayers seem to fall flat. In frustration, you remember the time when you merely whispered the Lord's name and His presence was immediately there, but now in the stillness you want to shout, "God, where are you?" Like Job, turning every way, you seek Him, yet you cannot perceive Him or His workings on your behalf.

Welcome to the wilderness! Know that you are not alone, but in good company.

You walk where Moses walked . . . Moses, raised in Pharaoh's court as a prince; Moses, with the vision of delivering his people out of bondage and slavery; Moses, who watched sheep on the back side of the desert for forty years.

You are alongside Joseph . . . Joseph, the highly favored of his father; Joseph, who had dreams of leadership and achievement; Joseph, thrown in a pit by his own brothers, then sold as a slave and later locked in prison.

You are sitting beside Job . . . Job, the man whom the Bible describes as "the greatest of all the men of the east" (Job 1:3); Job, who lost everything—possessions, children, health, the support of his wife.

Most importantly, you are accompanied by the Son of God—Jesus, who after receiving the public witness of God the Father and the Holy Spirit that He was, indeed, the Son of God, walked into the wilderness to face the forces of darkness.

The procession of wilderness travelers is long, for the wilderness is a necessary time, a season in the life of every child of God. We wish it could be bypassed; we watch for a shortcut or detour, but there isn't one. It's the route to the promised land, and the promised land cannot be attained without passing through the wilderness. Our understanding of this time or season is imperative if we are to make it to the promised land.

UNDERSTANDING THE TIMES

> . . . The sons of Issachar . . . had under-
> standing of the times, to know what Israel
> ought to do; . . .   I Chronicles 12:32 (NKJV)

Because they **understood** the timing of God, the sons of Issachar knew what Israel ought to do. Those who understand the times and seasons of the Spirit will know what God wants to accomplish and will respond wisely. Conversely, those without the **understanding** of God's times and seasons will **not** know what He is trying to accomplish in their lives and will act unwisely. Explaining this, Jesus said in Luke 12:54-56:

> Whenever you see a cloud rising out of the west, immediately you say, A shower is coming; and so it is. And when you see the south wind blow, you say, There will be hot weather; and there is. Hypocrites! You can discern the face of the sky and of the earth, but how is it you do not **discern this time**?
> [Emp. added]   Luke 12: 54-56 (NKJV)

Can a farmer *harvest* during the season of planting? Obviously, the answer is "no." If he does not *plant* in the season of sowing, he will not *reap* at the time of harvest. And planting at the correct time is crucial to his crop. If a farmer plants too early or too late, it will diminish his yield at harvest time. The seeds will not be in the proper position to receive what they need to flourish. The rain and heat, snow and cold will come before the seeds are ready. In order for *his crop* to benefit fully from God's provision, a farmer must understand thoroughly his season of sowing. Presently in the Church, we are in the process of preparing for the coming harvest; in order for *us* to benefit fully from God's pruning and care, we must recognize the season. We cry out for harvest, yet it is not the season of harvest, but of pruning and grafting.

Jesus rebuked the multitudes because they looked for the wrong thing at the wrong **time**. For:

> To everything there is a season, a time for every purpose under heaven: ...
> Ecclesiastes 3:1 (NKJV)

In this book we hope to share understanding of a particular season with a crucial purpose . . . it is the wilderness season, a time of pruning and grafting. Its purpose: preparation.

The wilderness is not a negative time for those who obey God. Its purpose is very positive: to train and prepare us for a new move of His Spirit. Unknowingly, when entering the wilderness, many behave without wisdom. Without understanding, they search for and do the wrong things. If you search for an escape route before understanding why God has you in a particular situation, i.e., wilderness, you unwittingly will prolong your wilderness time. This can cause you to experience hardship, frustration, and even defeat, because you don't understand the season nor the place to which God has led you. This was the case of the children of Israel. **Lack of understanding of their wilderness time** caused an entire generation to be unfit to inherit the promised land. God's purpose in leading them to the wilderness was to test, train, and prepare them to be sanctified warriors. But instead, the children of Israel erroneously perceived the wilderness as punishment, so they murmured, complained, and lusted constantly. When the time came for them to leave the wilderness and conquer and occupy the promised land, they heeded the evil report of murmurers and complainers. Given the choice between God's promises and His ability and man's perceptions and inability, they chose to believe man rather than God. They believed they were unable to receive their land flowing with milk and honey, so God said, "Okay, it will be as you believed." *Augh*

> These things happened to them as examples, and they were written for our instruction, . . .   I Corinthians 10:11 (NKJV)

Their ignorance of God's nature and character caused them to act wickedly, and what was to have been a brief wilderness journey became a lifetime experience.

Those with understanding of the wilderness will enter in with joy, knowing that beyond this place a "promised land" waits for them. This joy, from the vision set before them, will be the strength they need to finish the journey, that they might "Be perfect [mature] and complete, lacking nothing" (James 1:4).

God is creating able vessels for His use, ready for the fresh move of His Spirit.

THE WILDERNESS: NOT A TIME OF PUNISHMENT OR DISAPPROVAL

This book will discuss what the wilderness *is*, and what it *is not*—its purpose, its benefits, and its judgment. It is my prayer that, by these examples, illustrations, and words of instruction which the Holy Spirit has compelled me to share, you will see how to walk wisely in this land and season of wilderness.

Let us begin with Jesus as an example of one who successfully completed the wilderness training.

In Luke 3:22, the Holy Spirit descended upon Jesus in manifest form (a dove) and the voice of the Father proclaimed, "You are my beloved son; in You **I am well pleased.**" Not only did God proclaim Jesus as His Son, but He announced for all to hear that He approved of Him. Yet we find in Luke 4:1, "Jesus being filled with the Holy Spirit . . . was led by the spirit into the wilderness." This should make it clear to us that the reason for being led into the wilderness is *not* the disapproval or punishment of God. It is important that this is absolutely clear at the beginning of this book. It is imperative that this question is settled in our hearts!

Another point that must be understood clearly is that God didn't bring you to the wilderness to abandon you to Satan's devices and forget about you. God exhorted the second generation children of the exodus before entering into the promised land: "And you shall remember that the Lord your God **led you all the way these forty years in the wilderness . . .**" [Emp. added] (Deuteronomy 8:2 NKJV). Don't be misinformed—the Lord does not stop working in our lives just because we are in the wilderness. He leads us *through* it; without Him we could never make it through. Furthermore, it is *not* a place in which we are "put on a shelf" until He desires to use us. That is not the way our Father, who loves us, operates. On the contrary, it is a place and time during which He works mightily. You are familiar with the expression, "You can't see the forest for the trees"; well, the wilderness is much the same—it is difficult to see God moving when you are in the midst of it.

The third point that must be clear is this: the wilderness is not a place of defeat, at least **not to those who obey God.** Jesus—weak from hunger, with no human in whom to confide or from whom to receive encouragement, and without physical comfort or supernatural manifestation for forty days—was attacked by the devil in the wilderness. Jesus defeated him with the Word of the Lord! The wilderness is not a time when God's children are defeated. "Now thanks be to God who **always** leads us in **triumph in Christ** . . ." [Emp. added] (II Corinthians 2:14).

While the people of Israel sojourned in the wilderness, they were harassed by the nations of that area. The Lord told Israel to fight back. The children of Israel defeated the Amorites (Numbers 21:21-25), the Midianites (Numbers 31:1-11), and the people of Bashan (Numbers 21:33-35). If God's purpose was for them to experience defeat, He would not have told them to defend their position. However, though it wasn't intended as a time of defeat, many died without entering the promised land. This was not the way God desired it to be, but the sad result of their disobedience.

I hope this settles in your heart that the reason behind the wilderness is **not** the disapproval or punishment of God. Nor is it a place in which God abandons and forgets about you. It will be a place of victory when we believe and obey God!

CHAPTER 2

DEFINING THE WILDERNESS

The time now comes when character must be developed. And the wilderness is where it is done . . .

In the previous chapter we determined what the wilderness is **not**. In this chapter we will shed light on what it **is**. Many come under self-condemnation upon entering this time period. They think they have missed God or somehow displeased Him. But they have misunderstood the meaning or purpose of the wilderness. In the Bible and throughout history, men and women have gone through the wilderness as a time of preparation for their destiny in God. **So the wilderness is not God's rejection but His preparation.**

At the onset of this book I would like to remind you that the events in the Old Testament are examples and foreshadowings of the New Testament and covenant. I will use Old Testament events and prophecies to illustrate the wilderness. Only through incorporating the law and the prophets into our studies can we fully understand how God works and deals with His Church. Jesus said in Matthew 5:17-18, "Think not that I am come to destroy the **law,** or the **prophets**: I am not come to destroy, but to **fulfil**." The Holy Spirit illumi-

nates the scriptures, revealing the mysteries of the Old
Testament hidden in Christ. In reading the Old Testament
you will see the truths of the New Testament exemplified. I
Corinthians 10:11 (NKJV) says:

> Now all these things happened to them
> as examples, and they were written for our
> instruction, upon whom the ends of the ages
> have come.

In other words, God wants us to benefit from the lessons
and lives of the patriarchs and prophets. Even though
many Old Testament prophecies have seen historic fulfillment, this does not negate their application in current
times. One does not invalidate the other.

PERCEPTION OF THE WILDERNESS

Let's look at an Old Testament example of the wilderness described in the book of Job.

> Look, I go forward, but **He [is] not there,**
> and backward, but **I cannot perceive Him;**
> when He works on the left hand, I cannot
> behold Him; when He turns to the right
> hand, I cannot see Him. But He knows the
> way that I take; when He has tested me, I
> shall come forth as gold. [Emp. added]
> Job 23:8-10 (NKJV)

What a classic description of the wilderness. Job searches for
the presence and moving of God in his life. Yet the more he
searches, the more elusive God seems. God, however, is working on Job's behalf and knows exactly what is happening in
Job's life. So just because God's presence is not readily notice-
able, it does not mean He is not there and working in our lives.

When you first received the Lord Jesus and were filled with the Holy Spirit, God's presence was wonderfully real to you. You would call His name and instantly He responded. When you prayed, He manifested His presence. As a newborn child in His family you received the attention given a baby.

When children are newborn, they require constant care. They must be fed, clothed, and bathed, and they rely on others to do everything for them. However, as children grow, they must be allowed to mature. When our oldest son began to feed himself, he became frustrated because he couldn't put his food in his mouth as quickly or efficiently as his mommy. Now he struggled to receive what once had come so easily. Many times it would have been easier for all of us if we had continued feeding him, instead of allowing him to do it for himself. However, if we had taken the "easy" way, his maturing in this area would have been hindered greatly. As babies grow, the level of assistance they receive changes to encourage growth and development.

God does this with us so we can develop and mature spiritually. When we are newly born again and filled with His Spirit, for a season He manifests Himself at our every cry. In order to foster maturity, He allows us to go through times in which He does not respond instantly to our every call.

The time comes when character must be developed. And the wilderness is where it is done . . . the wilderness where God appears to be miles away and His promises even farther. He is, however, close at hand, for He has promised never to leave nor forsake us (Hebrews 13:5).

It is a time when you appear to be going in the opposite direction of your dreams and the promises He made. You perceive no growth and development. In fact, you may feel you are regressing. His presence seems to diminish, rather than grow. You may feel unloved and even ignored. But you are not.

DAILY BREAD

This is a time when God gives you "daily bread," not "abundance of things"—a time when you get what you **need** physically or materially, rather than what you **want**. It is a time that you experience socially what you **need**, not what you **want**. In the wilderness God knows what you **need** spiritually, and it may not be what you **think you need**! In America, we call this **lack** and say, "Lack is of the devil." The problem is that *our* definition of **needs** and **wants** differs from reality. We call our wants "needs," when this is not so!

The American Church has yet to learn what Paul meant in Philippians 4:11-13 (AMP):

> Not that I am implying that I was in any personal want, for I have learned how to be **content** (satisfied to the point where I am not disturbed or disquieted) in whatever state I am. **I know how to be abased and live humbly in straitened circumstances, and I know also how to enjoy plenty and live in abundance.** I have learned in **any and all circumstances** the secret of facing every situation, whether well-fed or going hungry, having a **sufficiency and to spare** or going without and being in want. **I have strength for all things in Christ Who empowers me.** . . . [Emp. added]

Paul learned through the strength of Christ that he could be as content in dry times as he was in abundance. We have learned neither in the Church of America! Sadly, those with abundance are no more content than those who suffer lack of abundance.

If we do not possess all we feel is rightly ours, we call it "lack." We judge men's faith and measure their spirituality by what they possess, when what we should see is their character. The children of Israel left Egypt with great possessions plundered from the Egyptians—articles of silver and gold and fine apparel. But they used the precious metals to build idols in the desert, then adorned themselves in fine apparel and danced before them. Yet these possessions did not indicate godliness—in fact, it appears the opposite was true. Only two of the original members of the exodus had the character to enter and possess the promised land. Only Joshua and Caleb entered, because they had a different spirit—they followed God fully! (Numbers 14:24). Our value system is warped if we measure one another by the standard of what we have and not who we are.

On the other hand, many times when a Christian comes into abundance financially, or perhaps a position of leadership or influence, he views it as God's permission to do as he wishes! He buys whatever he wants, spending the money on his own lusts (desires), or uses his position of influence to his benefit. In actuality, financial blessing and greater authority should bring greater dependence on God for His purpose or leading.

Some, when put in a position of authority, see it as a vehicle to serve *their* agenda, not God's. They abuse God's people to fulfill their own desires. Paul, though he had authority to receive financial support from churches through sowing to them spiritually, said, "If we have sown spiritual things for you, is it a great thing if we reap your material things? If others are partakers of this right over you, are we not even more? **Nevertheless we have not used this right,** but endure all things lest we hinder the gospel of Christ." [Emp. added] (I Corinthians 9:11-12, NKJV). That the gospel not be hindered was more important to Paul than receiving what was rightfully his.

Paul said in writing to the Philippians regarding their offering, "Not that I seek the gift, but I seek the fruit that abounds to your account." (Philippians 4:17, NKJV). His concern was the welfare of the people who gave, not his own personal benefit nor that of his ministry.

Some have not learned to abound in the anointing. They use it to build crowds and ministry. Their motive: to make a name for themselves, or possibly a large offering. Whatever it is, if the focus is not the heart of God, it will bring destruction. God's heart is for the people, not a minister's selfish motives. That is why we are admonished in Philippians 2:3-5 (NKJV):

> Let **nothing** be done through **selfish ambition** or **conceit**, but in **lowliness of mind** let each esteem others better than himself. Let each of you look out not only for his own interests, but also for the interests of others. Let **this mind be in you which was also in Christ Jesus,** . . . [Emp. added]

This was the attitude of Jesus in His ministry. He was not selfishly motivated. He took upon Himself our sin, sickness, and the death penalty (thus esteeming our welfare more important than His own), even though **He was innocent.** His purpose for life and ministry was not self-serving but self-giving! Through denying Himself, He gave the greatest gift of all—eternal life.

Such maturity of character is developed in us by God when we are in the wilderness. The wilderness is where the fruit of the Spirit is cultivated. Watered by the intense desire to know Him, we seek to walk as He walks. Paul's goal was not to build a huge ministry, but to know the Lord Jesus intimately and, above all else, to please Him!

The wilderness is a dry place. It may be dry spiritually, financially, socially, or physically. It is here that God gives "daily bread," not "abundance of things." He meets our needs in this time—not necessarily our wants. The purpose of the wilderness: to purify us. Our pursuit is to be His *heart*, not His *provision*. Then when we come into abundant times, we won't forget that it was the Lord, our God, Who gave us abundance in order to establish **His covenant** (Deuteronomy 8:2-18).

SECTION 2

TIME OF TESTING

CHAPTER 3

TIME OF TESTING

Often, even today, we seek Jesus for the wrong reasons. We unknowingly use Him. He is reduced to a resource in time of need.

> . . . The Lord your God led you . . . in the wilderness, to humble you and to test you, to know what was in your heart, . . .
> Deuteronomy 8:2 (NKJV)

Picture this: You are an Israelite, recently freed after a lifetime of slavery. You just experienced the frightening, yet exhilarating walk between two walls of swirling, angry waters to come out safe and dry on the other side. You turned to watch as those same walls which gave protection to you closed in death on your enemies. You joyously celebrated and danced at God's victorious deliverance! You feel invincible, knowing God is on your side. You never will doubt again One so mighty and faithful!

But now the scene is different: it is a few days later—you are tired, thirsty, and hot. You are not at the threshold of this "promised" land; instead, you are wandering aimlessly in a desert filled with serpents and scorpions. Now you are not

so said why was s allowed to live through these surgerys to end up where am now

dancing and singing to the Lord about the horse and its rider thrown into the sea, but complaining to your leader saying, "Why have you brought us out of Egypt? To kill us and our children and our livestock with thirst?"

Now, let's look at you! Do you believe God mightily delivered you from the power of the enemy to leave you wandering aimlessly through a desert of confusion and silence? Was this His purpose?

Just as the Lord led the children of Israel out of Egypt into the wilderness, so He leads you. The devil did not lead you, God did. And there is a purpose for these dry times. First, He humbles us, then He tests us. He does this so we can know the *true* nature of our hearts.

How does He humble? "So He humbled you, **allowed you to hunger, and fed you with manna** . . ." [Emp. added] (Deuteronomy 8:3, NKJV). He humbled the Israelites by allowing them to hunger. But His next statement declares He fed them with manna. It sounds contradictory. How could He cause them to hunger while feeding them manna?

Now, manna is the best food you can eat. It is what angels eat. Elijah was strengthened for a forty-day journey on two cakes of it. And the Israelites had an abundance of it. They received a fresh shipment from heaven every morning. *They never missed a meal* . . . from the day God started the manna until they camped on the shores of the promised land.

So why did God say, "I caused you to hunger?" What hunger is He speaking of? To understand, consider their situation. Let's say all you had for breakfast was a loaf of bread, and every evening all you had for dinner was a loaf of bread. No butter, no peanut butter, no jelly, no cold cuts, no tuna fish, *just bread.*

Now, we're not just talking a few days or weeks, but *forty years* of this diet.

When I was a youth pastor, we took fifty-six young people to the nation of Trinidad for an eight-day mission trip. The church in Trinidad prepared our meals. They were gracious, but every day we ate chicken. They prepared it many different ways and served it with rice and vegetables, but still it was always chicken.

After eight days of chicken, we hungered for something else. Upon returning home, one of the young men in our group asked his mother what was for dinner, and she replied, "Chicken." He begged her to take him for a hamburger.

Now, we were whining after only eight days; can you imagine forty years? Not four years but forty! We now see how God caused them to hunger. He didn't give them the things their flesh **wanted**. He only gave them what their flesh **needed**.

What else caused them to hunger? We get excited about the fact that their clothes and shoes didn't wear out. Well, how would you like to wear the same wardrobe for forty years? Have you thought how outdated their forty-year-old outfits looked? No new clothes, no shopping malls, and no department stores . . . the same shoes and accessories—nothing new for forty years!

They had what they **needed**—protection from heat and cold—but not what they **wanted**.

How else did they hunger? They saw the same scenery, day after day, for forty years. Every day brought cactus, bullrushes, and dry, parched ground; no streams, forests, or beautiful lakes . . . just desert.

In light of this, let's reexamine this verse:

> So He humbled you, allowed you to hunger, and fed you with manna . . . that He might make you know that man shall not live by bread alone; but man lives by every word that proceeds from the mouth of the Lord.   Deuteronomy 8:3 (NKJV)

What did God do? He created hunger by removing anything that would have satisfied the desires and wants of their flesh, while still meeting their fundamental needs.

He created this hunger to test them. What was this test? He wanted to see if they would desire Him instead of what they had left behind; to see if they would seek Him or what their flesh craved; to see if they would hunger and thirst for righteousness or for comfort and pleasure!

This was their response:

> Now the mixed multitude who were among them **yielded to intense craving;** so the children of Israel also wept again and said: **Who will give us meat to eat?**
> **We remember the fish which we ate freely in Egypt,** the cucumbers, the melons, the leeks, the onions, and the garlic; but now our whole being is dried up; there is nothing at all except this manna before our eyes. [Emp. added]   Numbers 11:4-6 (NKJV)

They remembered what they had left behind in Egypt (an example of the world's system). Their condition in Egypt, even with its bondage, now appeared preferable to the dry place into which God had led them.

They began to complain and murmur, crying out for meat. God heard their cry:

> And He gave them **their request,** so they ate (meat—quail) and were well filled, for **He gave them their own desire.** They were not deprived of their craving; But (He) **sent leanness into their soul.** [Emp. added]
>   Psalms 106:15; 78:29-30 (NKJV)

They got what they wanted, but at a high price. With this meat came "leanness of soul." This leanness **made them unfit to endure, unable to pass God's test, and ultimately, they never entered His PROMISED LAND!** The sin wasn't in the request for meat, but what that request represented. It revealed the dissatisfaction of their hearts with God and His method of leading, as well as their intense desire for the former things, which they remembered as pleasant, in spite of their captivity.

Currently, God has brought His Church into the wilderness. Spiritually, America is a dry and thirsty land. Our time of testing is at hand. **God once again watches to see whether His people will seek His *face* or His *hand*. His face represents His character and nature; it denotes a *relationship*. His hand represents His *provision* and *power*. If you seek only His hand, you may not recognize His face. But if you know the face, you will know His hand.**

The Pharisees did not recognize God's face in the person of Jesus; they were watching only for His hand to deliver them from Roman bondage. Let us not be like them.

If our heart is after God, if we will love, obey, and seek Him, even in these "dry times," He will raise up forerunners. Like Joshua, they will arise and take the "Promised Land," partaking in the harvest of the nations.

God is raising up a "Joshua Generation," but as in Joshua's time, the army's training ground is the wilderness. These dry times sift the murmurers, the complainers, and the rebellious, just as the wheat is separated from the chaff.

Those seeking only the benefits of the promise and not the "Promiser" Himself will faint in the dry desert places. It is one thing to seek the Lord for what He can give you or do for you. It is quite another to seek the Lord for *Who He is.* The first is for your benefit; the motive, selfish. At best, an immature relationship will develop from this motivation. But seeking the Lord for Who and what He is will build a strong and healthy relationship.

MOTIVE FOR SEEKING

On the following day, when the people . . .
saw that Jesus was not there, nor His disci-

ples, they also got into boats and came to
Capernaum, **seeking Jesus.** And when they
found Him on the other side of the sea, they
said to Him, Rabbi, when did You come here?
  Jesus answered them and said, Most
assuredly, I say to you, **you seek Me,** not
because you saw the signs, but because you
ate of the loaves and were filled. [Emp.
added]   John 6:22-26 (NKJV)

The multitudes of people came **seeking Jesus.** When
they finally found Him, He looked at them and said the reason wasn't because of the signs they saw, but because they
had eaten and were filled. Now, what do signs do? They
give direction or information. A sign never points to itself.
It directs you or gives information. Jesus knew they weren't
seeking Him because of the signs and miracles, which
pointed to Him as the Messiah, but only so their stomachs
would be filled.

Often, even today, we seek Jesus for the wrong reasons.
We pursue only His benefits and blessings, rather than pursue Him out of love. We unknowingly use Him. He is
reduced to a resource in time of need.

Have you ever had a person who contacts you only
when he needs or wants something from you? Or even
worse, have you ever had a person seek friendship with
you only to find out later their motive was to gain something you have? Perhaps it was your influence, money,
material goods, or position? There was no genuine concern or love for you, but for a time you served their purpose. If you've experienced this, you know how it feels to
be used.

This selfish attitude has permeated society, as well as
the Church. This mindset is why divorce is at an all-time
high. Even in the Church, couples marry for selfish reasons. They fail to realize marriage is a covenant of love,
not a contract. They marry because of what their partner

can do for them. And if this partner fails to meet their
expectations, they seek another, ignoring the fact that in
God's eyes a covenant is far stronger and more binding
than a contract.

Many in the Church are discontented, their love cold.
Some backslide; others depart from the faith. They serve
the Lord for what He can do for them, not out of love for
Who He is. So, as long as God provides their *wants*, they are
happy and excited about Him. But upon entering dry
times, **the motive of their hearts is revealed.** Anytime the
focus is *self*, complaining will begin.

This is illustrated once again by the children of Israel.
When the Lord delivered them from the hand of the
Pharaoh, the people rejoiced.

> Then Miriam the prophetess, the sister of
> Aaron, took the timbrel in her hand; and all
> the women went out after her with timbrels
> and with dances. And Miriam answered them:
> Sing to the Lord, for He has triumphed
> gloriously! The horse and its rider He has
> thrown into the sea!
> Exodus 15:20-21 (NKJV)

They were overwhelmed by His greatness and miraculous power. Their hearts were filled with excitement
because of His deliverance. Yet only three days later, in the
wilderness of Shur, they encountered bitter waters and the
complaining began:

And the people complained against Moses, saying,
"What shall we drink?" (Exodus 15:24). Couldn't the same
God who parted the Red Sea make bitter waters become
sweet? Wasn't Moses the same leader who had been a hero
three days earlier? God did, indeed, change the bitter
waters to sweet. Then a few days later, they were complaining because of the food. They murmured saying, "It was
better for us before God delivered us."

> Then the whole congregation of the chil-
> dren of Israel complained against Moses
> and Aaron in the wilderness.
>
> And the children of Israel said to them,
> Oh that we had died by the hand of the Lord
> in Egypt, when we sat by the pots of meat
> and when we ate bread to the full ... !
>
> Exodus 16:2-3 (NKJV)

Now their complaints were directed at Moses and
Aaron. But in verse 8, Moses tells the truth of the matter:
"Your complaints are not against us but against the Lord"
[Emp. added] (Exodus 16:8, NKJV).

In the dry times, when complaining begins, it will usually be directed at leadership, family, or friends. Most of us
(out of fear) would never speak against God directly, by
name. Why did they complain against Moses and Aaron,
(and thus the Lord)? In *their* eyes, He had disappointed
them.

God is weighing the heart of the Church in America.
May we seek Him now, so that our hearts will not be found
wanting.

CHAPTER 4

OUR EXAMPLE

We struggle under the heavy weight of unfulfilled vows and promises, until we are so burdened we can barely lift our voice in prayer.

Moreover, brethren, I do not want you to be unaware that **all** our fathers were under the cloud, **all** passed through the sea, **all** were baptized into Moses in the cloud and in the sea, **all** ate the same spiritual food, and **all** drank the same spiritual drink. For they drank of that spiritual Rock that followed them, and that Rock was Christ. [Emp. added]
I Corinthians 10:1-4 (NKJV)

Paul points out that **all** were *covenant* children, descendants of Abraham, not gentiles. They all traveled under the cloud of God's protection, were baptized into Moses, who was a foreshadowing of Christ, our Deliverer. And all partook of the spiritual food and drink of Christ. So it is clear we are viewing a nation of people which foreshadows that of the New Testament Christian. Paul stressed the word "all" five times, as if to say, "We aren't talking about any heathen here." He goes on to say:

27

But with **most** of them God was not well pleased, for their bodies were scattered in the wilderness. Now these things became our **examples,** . . . [Emp. added]
                                    I Corinthians 10:5-6 (NKJV)

How did most displease God? Here are the five major reasons:

1. They lusted after evil things.
2. They pursued idols.
3. They committed acts of sexual immorality.
4. They tempted the Lord.
5. They complained against the Lord.

After listing these, Paul goes on to say: "Now all these things happened to them as **examples,** and they were written for **our instruction,** upon whom the ends of the ages have come" [Emp. added] (I Corinthians 10:11 NKJV).

If this is written for **our** instruction, it is imperative we understand! The five areas of sin were just manifestations (or the bad fruit) of a deeper *root* problem. The author of Hebrews describes the same thing and gives an explanation for these five acts of disobedience.

> Wherefore I was grieved with that generation, and said, **They do alway err in their heart;** and **they have not known my ways.** [Emp. added]   Hebrews 3:10

The error was in their heart, which produced evil actions! If your heart is right, your actions inevitably will line up. Without a correct heart, you will fall short of His calling. Your focus must be to hit the **mark of the high call of God, to know Him.** A wrong focus will hit the wrong target.

Paul said in Philippians 3:13-14:

Brethren, **I count not myself to have**

> **apprehended**: but this one thing I do, forget-
> ting those things which are behind, and
> reaching forth unto those things which are
> before, **I press toward the mark for the
> prize of the high calling of God in Christ
> Jesus.** [Emp. added]

In order to achieve the high call of God for our lives, we first must acknowledge the fact that we haven't yet attained it, that we are not perfected and must continue to pursue, change, and grow.

Many reach a comfort zone or plateau where they begin to "maintain" rather than "press in." They set their personal standards by comparing themselves with others, or by what they feel is adequate. At this point, they stop seeking God for who He is and begin to pursue the bene-fits. Their focus is "off," and they begin to **err in their hearts**. They may seek to build their status or their posi-tions in the church, or perhaps they wish to increase their comfort or popularity. Their emphasis will turn from God to self.

God was not the pursuit of the children of Israel. Therefore, they were unable to know His ways. They got excited about His mighty works—who wouldn't? They rejoiced at every marvelous miracle, *because it benefited them.* The focus was themselves. Whenever God's super-natural power was not manifested, they strayed. If Moses was on the mountain, they played. They were satisfied with merely the benefits of salvation. There was no longing for more of God. They did not press in to know God in an inti-mate relationship.

One day in the wilderness, God told Moses to go down and tell the people to consecrate themselves, for He was coming to Mount Sinai to speak to them, just as He had spoken to Moses. However, when the day came and the Lord manifested His presence with rumblings and thun-derings in the sight of Israel, the people fled:

> And all the people saw the thunderings,
> and the lightnings, and the noise of the
> trumpet, and the mountain smoking: and
> when the people saw it, they removed, and
> **stood afar off.** And **they said unto Moses,
> Speak thou with us, and we will hear: but
> let not God speak with us, lest we die.**
> [Emp. added]   Exodus 20:18

They pleaded with Moses: "You talk to God for us and tell
us what He says, and we will do it . . . ," (paraphrased) again
manifesting their desire for only gain, without a *relationship*.
They had good intentions—they intended to keep God's
word, but without a *relationship* they couldn't. How can you
remain faithful to someone you don't know or spend time
with? They wanted a formula instead of a relationship, so
God gave them the Ten Commandments. Yet, generation
after generation they proved that they were unable to keep
these commandments. God knew they would be unable to
keep these laws hewn on stone unless somehow He could
replace their hearts of stone with His law.

And now we turn to the Church today. How many of us
with the best of intentions try to keep the laws of God? We
struggle under the heavy weight of unfulfilled vows and
promises, until we are so burdened we can barely lift our
voices in prayer. We look to the minister, our mates, or our
friends, hoping they will seek God on our behalf and tell us
what He is saying. Like the children of Israel, we try to keep
His commandments without maintaining a life-giving relationship with the Lord. We err in our hearts! Jesus said in
John 14:21:

> He that hath my commandments, and
> keepeth them, **he it is that loveth me:** and he
> that loveth me shall be loved of my Father,
> and I will love him, and **will manifest
> myself to him.** [Emp. added]

I used to read that scripture and think the Lord said, "John, if you keep my commandments, you will prove that you love me." Then one day the Lord told me to read that scripture again. So I read it again. He said, "You did not get what I was saying—read it again." This went on till I read the scripture ten times. Finally, I said, "Lord forgive my ignorance; show me what You're saying!" He said, "John, I wasn't saying if you keep my commandments, you prove you love me. I already know whether you love me or not! What I was saying was, if a man falls head over heels in love with me, he will be the one enabled to keep my commandments!" It is a relationship, not law. The way I viewed it was law. What He revealed was the importance of a *relationship*. God can't be known through rules and regulations. God can't be found in methods. The Holy Almighty One cannot be reduced to a formula! Yet this is the perception many have of the Lord. In place of their relationship with God they have substituted the seven steps to healing, four-point plan of salvation, five scriptures on prosperity, and the baptism of the Holy Spirit. They imagine God is somehow contained in their box of promises, to be pulled and claimed as they feel necessary. They wonder why they have so much trouble with sin! Why do they find His commandments so hard to keep? It is because they err in their hearts!

Let's illustrate to make it clearer. Have you ever fallen in love? When I was engaged to my wife, Lisa, I was head over heels in love with her. I thought of her constantly. I'd do whatever was necessary to spend as much time with her as possible. If she needed something, no matter what I was doing, I would jump in my car and get it for her. I didn't have to force myself to talk to people about her ... I extolled her praises to anyone who would listen.

Because of my intense love for her, it was a joy for me to do whatever she wished. I didn't do these things to *prove* I loved her; I did them *because* I loved her. Just a few short years into our marriage, I turned my attention to other things, such as the work of the ministry. It was now bothersome to do something

for her. Taken for granted, Lisa was not in my thoughts as
much. Gifts for her came only out of obligation on Christmas,
anniversaries, and birthdays . . . and even that was a bother.
Our marriage was in trouble. Our first love was dying! Because
the intensity of our original love was no longer there, now it
was difficult to do things for her. Since then, God turned my
heart and let me see how selfish I had become. Graciously, He
rekindled the flames of our love and healed our marriage.

In light of this, you can understand why Jesus said:

> Nevertheless I have somewhat against
> thee, because thou hast **left thy first love.**
> Remember therefore from whence thou art
> fallen, and repent, and do the first works; or
> else I will come unto thee quickly, and will
> remove thy candlestick out of his place,
> except thou repent. [Emp. added]
>
> Revelation 2:4-5

Moses, on the other hand, was different from the children of Israel. He was not content to worship God from
afar. When he beheld the manifestation of God's presence,
he pressed in and drew near. Exodus 20:21 says, "And **the
people stood afar off,** and **Moses drew near unto the thick
darkness where God was.**" [Emp. added]

Even though Moses was a man with influence and power,
with a congregation of three million, who had been part of
the most astounding signs and wonders in the Old
Testament, he knew these alone would never satisfy him.
Examine his prayer after he had experienced all the incredi-
ble signs and wonders:

> Now therefore, I pray thee, if I have found
> grace in thy sight, **shew me now thy way, that
> I may know thee,** . . . And he [Moses] said
> unto him [the Lord], If thy presence go not
> with me, carry us not up hence . . . . And he

said, **I beseech thee, shew me thy glory.**
[Emp. added]   Exodus 33: 13-18

We hear the heart cry of Moses. "Lord, I will not be satisfied until I see Your glory, that I might know *you*!" (paraphrased). In order to know God, we must know his *ways*! He
reveals His ways to those seeking after His heart, not just His
power. **But those who know His heart will walk in His
power:** ". . . but the people that do **know their God** shall be
strong, and do exploits" [Emp. added] (Daniel 11:32).

When I first entered the ministry, nearly every morning I
spent one to two hours a day in prayer. My prayers went
something like this: "God, use me to save souls, use me to
heal the sick, use me to cast out devils." On and on I would
pray—the same things in different words. I felt so selfless as
I cried out to God for a large ministry. Then one day the
Lord spoke to me and said, "Son, your prayers are selfish."
I was taken aback by what He said. "What is your motive
for wanting to do these things?" He said, "All I hear from
you is 'Use ME to . . .'; you are the focus of the prayer." He
went on to say, "My purpose for creating you was not to
have you cast out devils or heal the sick. My purpose for
creating you was for fellowship." Then He showed me
something I will never forget . . . Judas cast out devils and
healed the sick! Yes, when Jesus sent out the twelve, He
sent all of them—including Judas, the one who later
betrayed Him. My focus was wrong. The goal of the high
call of God is to *know Jesus Christ* (Philippians 3:10).

A few years later, my wife was praying along the same
lines as she prepared for a meeting. So the Lord said to her,
"Lisa, I don't *use* people, I anoint them, I heal them, I trans-
form them, I conform them to my image, but I don't *use*
them." He continued by asking, "Lisa, have you ever been
used by a friend?" "Yes," she answered. The Lord asked,
"How did you feel?" She answered, "I felt betrayed!"

The Lord went on: "Many ministers have cried for me to
only use them. 'Use me to heal, use me to save.' So I did,

hoping all along for their hearts, but they became too busy with the ministry for that. They never bothered to learn my ways, so they built *their own* kingdoms. When troubles hit, they cried out for me but were offended when I did not answer their prayers because they never knew me. They felt used and became angry with me. They fell away because they did not know me."

What would you think of a woman whose only ambition was to produce children by her husband, with no interest in knowing him personally? She would only be intimate with him if it would produce children. It sounds absurd, yet it is not so different from us crying out to God for Him to "use us to get people saved," when we, ourselves, don't even have a relationship with Him. When we are intimate with God, children will come forth—just as a man with his wife. This is why God says in Daniel 11:32, ". . . but the people that do **know their God** shall be strong, and do exploits." [Emp. added]

So, then, these were the roots of the children of Israel's sins: lusting after evil things, pursuing idols, committing acts of sexual immorality, and tempting and complaining against the Lord. They were **not** seeking and pursuing the right thing. They sought the created, rather than the Creator.

Joshua is a good example of someone whose heart was correct in the wilderness. When Moses went up to Mt. Sinai, Joshua stayed at the mountain's foot. He wanted to get as close as possible to the presence of the Lord. When Moses met with God in the tabernacle, Joshua was there also, in order to be close to the presence of the Lord. Even when Moses was finished, Joshua remained. "And the LORD spake unto Moses face to face, as a man speaketh unto his friend. And he turned again into the camp: **but his servant Joshua, the son of Nun, a young man, departed not out of the tabernacle**" [Emp. added] (Exodus 33:11).

Now examine again what Paul said: "But with many of them God was not well pleased: for they were overthrown in the wilderness" (I Corinthians 10:5). Why were the children of Israel overthrown? Because their focus was on themselves, not on God. Looking at the book of Joshua (the story of the next generation that was allowed to take the promised land), you will see that the five areas of sin that plagued their parents did not manifest themselves as readily with the second generation in the wilderness. It did happen once with a man named Achan; however, the leadership and people immediately sought God to take care of it. The reason for the change in the second generation was that their focus was turned as a result of watching an entire generation die in the wilderness, just short of seeing God's promise fulfilled.

The wilderness reveals the motives of our heart—it separates the *selfish* from the *selfless*. Ask the Holy Spirit to sort and weigh the motives of your heart, separating those that would hold you back from those that will propel you forward. Then become a wise servant; seek those things which are beneficial to the *relationship*, knowing that the other things will follow as a result of a proper relationship with God.

SECTION 3

TIME OF
PURIFICATION

CHAPTER 5

THE HIGHWAY OF GOD

. . . God is not looking for an outward form of holiness; He wants an inward change of heart, . . .

A voice of one calling: in the desert prepare the way for the Lord; **make straight in the wilderness a highway for our God.** [Emp. added]   Isaiah 40:3 (NIV)

The wilderness is the location of God's highway. It is in the wilderness that the way is prepared. It is the **way or road to the high or exalted life**—the way God lives and thinks.

For My thoughts are not your thoughts, nor are your ways **My ways**, says the Lord. For as the heavens are higher than the earth, so are **My ways higher** than your ways, and My thoughts than your thoughts. [Emp. added]   Isaiah 55:8-9 (NKJV)

Few have walked this road. Yet now, God is preparing

many to journey upon it. We find this described in Isaiah 35:6, 8 (NKJV):

> . . . for waters shall burst forth in the **wilderness**, and streams in the **desert**. . . . A highway shall be there [the desert] and a road, and it shall be called the **highway of holiness**. [Emp. added]

It is in the wilderness that the highway of the Lord is prepared. That way is called holiness.

One of the definitions of holiness is "the state of being pure." Jesus said, "Blessed are the **pure in heart**, for they shall **see God**." [Emp. added] (Matthew 5:8) The way or method to the high life is holiness or a pure heart.

Jesus is not returning for an unholy or impure Church; He is coming for a Church without spot, wrinkle, or any such thing. Many of us have tried to attain holiness by obeying rules and regulations and have failed miserably. Like the Jews who tried to receive salvation by keeping the law and could not, even so, we are unable to walk in holiness by keeping rules and regulations. Many have restricted themselves with legalistic rulings regarding tangible things (i.e., no make-up, strict dress code, no television sets). All these outward limits are established in an attempt to obtain inward purity. But God is not looking for an outward form of holiness; He wants an inward change of your heart, for a pure heart will produce pure conduct. Jesus said in Matthew 23:26 (NKJV), ". . . first cleanse the inside of the cup and dish [the heart], that the outside of them may be clean also."

If your heart is pure, you will not desire to dress in a way that is seductive. A woman can have a dress on down to her ankles and still have a seductive attitude, while another woman can wear a pair of pants and have a pure heart.

A man can boast that he has never been divorced, yet lust in his heart for other women. Is this holiness?

If your heart is pure, a television in your home will not cause you to watch or desire any unedifying programs. Some try to say that if Christians have a television in their home, they are worldly. A piece of furniture or electronics in your home does not determine whether or not you are worldly; it is what is in your heart that makes that determination. You can have no TV in your home and lust after it in your heart. If your heart is pure, you will desire only what God desires.

The wilderness is one of the crucibles God uses to purify your motives and intentions. God is in the process of preparing our hearts prior to His return for His Church. The rest of the chapters in this section will deal with how the Lord will purify His Church prior to His second coming. The book of Malachi will be the primary text because Malachi was the last prophet before the New Testament times. He was commissioned to prophesy of the preparation and event of the first coming of the Lord to His temple.

Four hundred years later the fulfillment of the first coming began with John the Baptist crying in the wilderness, "Prepare the way of the Lord."

We are living in the time of the second coming of the Lord to His temple. We will see the parallels of the preparation of His people for the first and the second coming of the Lord. Both begin with the purification of His people in the wilderness.

CHAPTER 6

THE TRUE PROPHETIC

*The focus of the true prohetic
anointing deals with hearts, . . .*

Behold, I will send you **Elijah the prophet**
before the coming of the **great** and **dreadful**
day of the Lord. [Emp. added]
Malachi 4:5 (NKJV)

The great day of the Lord was His first coming, and John
the Baptist was **the "Elijah Prophet"** sent by God to prepare His way. His ministry was, "A voice of one calling: in
the desert prepare the way for the Lord" (Isaiah 40:3, NIV).
John's role was prophesied by the prophets of old. Jesus
described him as follows:

. . . what did you go out to see? A
prophet? Yes, I say to you, and **more than a
prophet**. For this is he of whom it is written:
Behold, I send My messenger before Your
face, who will prepare Your way before You.
Assuredly, I say to you, among those born of

women there has **not risen one greater** than
John the Baptist; . . . And if you are willing to
receive it, **he is Elijah** who is to come. [Emp.
added]

Matthew 11:9-14 (NKJV)

John was not the Elijah of I & II Kings reincarnated. The
text is not referring or limited to a mere man, but it
describes the true meaning of "Elijah." To explain, the word
Elijah comes from two Hebrew words: *El* and *Yahh, El*
meaning "strength" and *Yahh* meaning "Jehovah" or Lord.
Together they mean **"strength of Jehovah."** So what is actually being said of John the Baptist is that he went before
Jesus in the "strength of Jehovah."

The angel Gabriel described John's call as follows:

And he will **turn many of the children of
Israel to the Lord their God.** He will also go
before Him [the Lord] in the **spirit and
power of Elijah**, to turn the hearts of the
fathers to the children, and the disobedient
to the wisdom of the just, **to make ready a
people prepared for the Lord.** [Emp. added]

Luke 1:16-17 (NKJV)

The thrust of John's ministry was to turn the heart of Israel
back to God; his message: "Repent for the kingdom of heaven
is at hand" (Matthew 3:2). Repentance means a **change of
heart.** The children of Israel's actions were very religious, but
their hearts were far from God. Thousands attended synagogue faithfully, unaware of the true condition of their hearts.
So God raised up the prophet John to **expose the actual condition of their hearts.** John declared to the **multitudes,**
"Offspring of vipers! Who warned you to flee from the wrath
to come? Therefore bear fruits worthy of **repentance [a change
of heart], and do not begin to say to yourselves, 'We have
Abraham as our father . . .'"** [Emp. added] (Luke 3:7-8, RSV).

He exposed the deception in which their hearts were trusting. They believed they were justified because they were children of Abraham and by their faithful attendance of synagogue and payment of tithes. John was not sent to the gentiles, but to awaken the "lost sheep" of the house of Israel, to prepare them to receive Jesus.

Malachi also prophesied this "Elijah anointing" would come before the great (the Lord's first coming) and dreadful day of the Lord. This "dreadful or awesome" day of the Lord is His second coming. I believe we are **now** living in that day. Confirming Malachi's prophecy, Jesus said: "'Indeed, **Elijah is coming** first and will restore all things. But I say to you that **Elijah has come** already.' . . . then the disciples understood that he was speaking to them of John the Baptist" [Emp. added] (Matthew 17:11-13, RSV). Jesus spoke this after John was beheaded. Notice He refers to two different time periods of the Elijah anointing: future (**is coming**) and past (**has come**).

Prior to the second coming of Jesus Christ, once again God will raise a prophetic anointing. However, this time the mantle will not rest upon a single man but corporately on a company of prophets. In the book of Acts, Peter quoted the the prophet Joel:

> . . . Your **sons** and your **daughters** shall prophesy . . . and on My **menservants** and on My **maidservants** I will pour out My spirit in those days; and they shall **prophesy** . . . before the coming of the great and **awesome** day of the Lord. [Emp. added]
> Acts 2:17-20 (NKJV)

The definition of the Greek word for "prophesy" in the above verse is to speak under divine inspiration, to exercise the prophetic office, to foretell events.

Like John the Baptist, latter-day prophets will go to the lost or deceived sheep in the church structure, as well as those who have left by the "door of offense." Most folks who attend church feel they are ready for Jesus to return. Not unlike the religious leaders and people of John's time, they believe that by their works, church attendance, tithes, or good standing, once they pray the sinner's prayer, they are justified. They may believe they are justified, but the truth is **they're not ready** for His return. Their hearts still stray. Once again the prophetic message will come to us, "Repent [change your heart], for the day of the Lord is at hand." Exposing any deception, these prophets shall bring forth truth.

More than any other nation, America has poured billions of dollars into Christian tapes, literature, outreach, and television programming. We have more Bible schools, training centers, and churches than other nations. On the whole, we are more educated in Scriptures and church doctrine than any other country. **Yet, as a nation, our churches remain dry, void of God's true presence.** Sinners sit in our services unconvicted! Sin runs rampant in our congregations, while leadership tolerates it. **Why?!**

True repentance has not been brought to the people. The Greek word translated **repentance** in Matthew 3:8 is *metanoia*. It is defined as a real change of mind and attitude toward sin and its causes, not merely the consequences of it. **We have learned to sorrow over the consequences of sin without forsaking its nature.** Unfortunately, our rejection of sin does not occur because its very nature grieves God, but rather because we are **embarrassed** by its offspring or exposure in our lives.

The focus of the true prophetic anointing is to deal with hearts, not merely to give "personal prophecies" to individuals. A prophet sees the heart of man and foresees the plan of God. He calls for change and warns of pending judgment. He can come into a church and not say one "thus saith the Lord . . .", and yet, he will have prophesied (spoken by divine inspiration) the entire service. The whole atmosphere of the church is changed because the prophet of God has dealt with the motive, yielding **true repentance**. He proclaims a new, more accurate direction. The summary of His message, whether to a church or an individual, is, "Turn to the Lord; there is a new move of God coming!"

The office of a prophet is **not limited** to a service in which Christians stand up and are given "personal prophecies," although this happens in various instances. He may have a word for an individual, such as Agabus' word for Paul in Acts 21:10-11. This, however, is not the thrust of his ministry.

In the book of Acts, Silas, Paul's traveling companion, was a prophet (Acts 15:32). We don't see him going from church to church holding services and giving "personal prophecies." What we do see is him exhorting the brethren to serve the Lord.

Some call themselves "prophets" and go about giving "personal words;" yet, they do not have God's heart, and in some cases are **self-appointed**. Their words flow from their own hearts or, in some instances, from familiar spirits. These "words" may even seem right, but God has not sent these alleged prophets, nor filled their mouths.

> **I have not sent these prophets, yet they ran [self-appointed]. I have not spoken to them, yet they prophesied.** But if they had stood in My counsel, and had caused **My people** to hear My words, **then they would have turned them from their evil way** [the thrust of the prophetic anointing] **and from the evil of their doings.** [Emp. added]
> Jeremiah 23:21-22 (NKJV)

God also says about those who are "self-appointed": "... They speak a vision of their **own heart,** not from the mouth of the Lord" [Emp. added] (Jeremiah 23:16).

In the same chapter, God says that from these self-appointed prophets **pollution** is released into the land, and because of their prophecies God's people are made "worthless" (verses 15-16).

Always look for the motive behind the ministry. Is it drawing the people closer to God? Or is it making them more dependent on the "prophet" and his/her gifting?

One of the by-products of the counterfeit prophetic move is people running to and fro seeking to give or receive "a word." Their focus: SELF. Rather than turning to the Lord and seeking His face, forsaking their wicked ways, they look outside for answers.

Jesus tells us how to recognize the true and false prophet: "You will know them by their fruits" (Matthew 7:16, NKJV). The proof of good fruit is when people begin to outwardly manifest the inward change in their lives. We must develop discernment to distinguish between true and false motives . . . as well as true and false prophets!

Remembering the *purpose* for the restoration of the prophetic office will prepare our hearts to receive this office and its ministry gifting. These prophets will be the voice of one crying, "In the wilderness prepare the highway of holiness."

CHAPTER 7

THE LORD COMES TO HIS TEMPLE

We now stand at the threshold . . . as the Son of God exposes the hypocrisy of our own hearts and implants His compassion . . .

Behold, I send My messenger, and he will prepare the way before Me. And the Lord, who you seek, will **suddenly come to His temple.** [Emp. added]
Malachi 3:1 (NKJV)

As we have seen in the previous chapter, this messenger is the prophetic anointing that will prepare the way of the Lord. Malachi said that the Lord, whom you seek, will suddenly come **TO** His temple. His temple is the Church. Notice it does not say **FOR** His temple, but **TO** it. Before the Lord comes **FOR** His Church in rapture, He's coming **TO** His Church . . . for judgment, refinement, and revival. This is illustrated in the book of Hosea:

Come, and let us return to the Lord; for He has torn, but He will heal us; He has stricken, but He will bind us up.
Hosea 6:1 (NKJV)

This is the message carried by the prophets who are sent to prepare His way. Their message is, "Church, let us return to the Lord." What does it mean, "He has torn, but He will heal us"? That is judgment.

> For the time has come for **judgment** to
> **begin** at the **house of God** [the temple]; and
> if it begins with us first, what will be the end
> of those who do not obey the gospel of God?
>   Now If the righteous one is **scarcely** saved,
> where will the ungodly and the sinner appear?
> [Emp. added]   I Peter 4:17-18 (NKJV)

Before God can judge the nations, He first must judge His "holy nation" (I Peter 2:9). Before the children of Israel could enter the promised land and drive out the nations, God first judged His people in the wilderness. This is prophetic. Before we point our finger at the world and say, "Repent and be converted"; before we see the great harvest of these last days, God will purge first the sin so evident in the Church. **The Church is like Jonah.** We are asleep in the ship. Our disobedience has brought calamity. God is using the world to say, "Wake up, Church, there is sin in you," just as He used the heathen on the ship to wake up the prophet Jonah. The media networks, reporters, IRS, and others have seen the greed, covetousness, pride, and immorality in the Church. If you want to know how Christians should act and live, just ask the sinners; they frequently have a better grasp on it than we do, I'm sorry to say. And they cry out against our hypocrisy. It is time for us to "**Awake** to righteousness, and DO NOT SIN; for some do not have the knowledge of God. I speak this to **your shame**" [Emp. added] (I Corinthians 15:34, NKJV).

God dealt with the disobedience of the prophet by purging him in the belly of the whale. Jonah cried out to God in **repentance**. He said, "I have been cast out of your sight; Yet **I will look again toward your holy temple**" [Emp. added]

(Jonah 2:4, NKJV). Once his heart was right, he was empowered to fulfill his **calling** and able to preach repentance to a sin-steeped Ninevah.

The Church in America has followed signs. God's Word tells us the signs are supposed to follow the believer—it seems we have it somewhat backward. People pursue the gifts and anointing of the Spirit rather than the character and heart of God.

God says, "**Pursue** love, and **desire** spiritual gifts . . ." [Emp. added] (I Corinthians 14:1, NKJV). As mentioned before, the Church has turned that around. We have **pursued** spiritual gifts (or signs) and **desired** love! People will drive a thousand miles for a miracle service, but still not allow God to deal with the anger, bitterness, unforgiveness, strife, etc. in their hearts.

Recently, in a meeting, I saw people run to the front to receive ministry, and the Spirit of God spoke something to my heart that shook me to the core. He said, "A **wicked** and **adulterous** generation **seeks after a sign**, and no sign shall be given to it except the sign of the prophet Jonah" [Emp. added] (Matthew 16:4, NKJV). Let's look at these two conditions of "wicked" and "adulturous."

The wicked generation seeks signs for their own selfish benefit, not to draw closer to the God of signs.

In Acts 8 a man named Simon sought the power of God, but with impure motives:

> Then laid they [their] hands on them, and they received the Holy Ghost. And when Simon saw that through laying on of the apostles' hands the Holy Ghost was given, he offered them money, Saying, **Give me also this power**, that on whomsoever I lay hands, he may receive the Holy Ghost. But Peter said unto him, Thy money perish with thee, because thou hast thought that the gift of God may be purchased with money. Thou

hast neither part nor lot in this matter: for
thy heart is not right in the sight of God.
Repent therefore of this thy **wickedness,**
and pray God, if perhaps the thought of
thine heart may be forgiven thee. For I perceive that thou art in the **gall of bitterness,**
and [in] the bond of iniquity. [Emp. added]
Acts 8:17-23

Simon's pursuit was the *anointing* of God, not His *character.* There was bitterness in his heart, and he was bound by
iniquity. He had no intention of dealing with the flaws of
his heart. However, he was very excited about receiving the
anointing of God upon his life. He was so excited, he was
even willing to offer something of value for it. Yet even
under the guise of ministry, his true motive was to promote
himself. We are not to pursue the anointing; it is a gift
which cannot be earned or learned.

A gift is given; it is granted freely or it is not a gift. Nor
can we bribe God by our gifts or performance—He gives
out of compassion in response to need. When you are
under God's anointing, you quickly see the anointing is for
the sake of others, not yourself.

An adulterer is an individual who has a covenant relationship with one, and yet becomes involved with another.
The Church has pursued relations with the world unfaith-
fully, while boasting that all Her sins are washed away by
the blood of Her covenant with Jesus. She has become adulterous. "You ask and do not receive, because you ask amiss,
that you may spend it on **your pleasures. Adulterers** and
adulteresses! Do you not know that friendship with the
world is enmity with God?" [Emp. added] (James 4:3-4,
NKJV). It is spiritual adultery to pursue the pleasures and
gain of the world's system once your allegiance is to Jesus.

The Lord is in the process of bringing His Church to a
crisis of judgment, as with Jonah, to turn Her heart back in
true repentance.

For He who eats and drinks [the bread
and cup of the Lord] in an unworthy manner eats and drinks **judgment** to himself, not
discerning the Lord's body. For this reason
many are weak and sick among you, and
many sleep [are dead]. For if we would
judge ourselves, **we would not be judged.**
But when we are **judged,** we are **chastened
by the Lord,** that we may not be condemned
with the world. [Emp. added]
　　　　　　I Corinthians 11:29-32 (NKJV)

This goes much further than just eating bread and drinking grape juice in church with unconfessed sin in our lives.
There is no power in the bread and grape juice—it is in
what they represent. Jesus said in John 6:56-57 (NKJV):

He who eats My flesh and drinks My
blood **abides in Me, and I in him.**
As the living Father sent Me, and I live
because of the Father, so he who **feeds on
Me** will live because of Me. [Emp. added]

As you can see, eating the bread and drinking the juice is
an outward sign of an inward commitment. **Abide** in
Christ, feed on Him—He is our life source. Don't live off of
the pleasures of this world, but on every word that proceeds from the mouth of God. As true Christians, our diet is
not that on which the world dines. For, "... you cannot par-
take of the Lord's table and of the table of demons" (I
Corinthians 10:21, NKJV). Our true source of joy and life
must be Jesus, and Him only. Too many of the world's
methods have crept into the Church. Much of this worldliness now is considered "normal Christianity." This carnali-
ty has dulled our discernment. For this reason, **many** in the
Church are in crisis situations. They are weak, sick, and
some even die prematurely. The reason may be a poor diet,

caused by mixing the Lord's table with the world's. One cuisine weakens the benefit of the other until they cancel each other out.

Now let me insert this very important statement. Just because a Christian is weak, sick, or dies young doesn't necessarily mean there is sin in his or her life. Paul said this is the reason for **many**, not in every case. Besides, we in the Church must take responsibility for an attitude of worldliness. We must not point fingers at individuals, which breeds a critical and judgmental spirit, but we must examine ourselves. Notice what God says: "For if we would judge [Greek: *diakrino*] ourselves we would not be judged [Greek: *krino*]." The first word "judge" means to separate thoroughly, as, when we examine **ourselves** thoroughly and remove the **vile** from the **precious**. The second means to punish or condemn. He goes on to say: "But when we are **judged** [Greek: *krino* – to punish or condemn], **we are chastened by the Lord, that we may not be condemned with the world.**" This is the mercy of God. He does not want us to be condemned with the world, so He will judge us first, which, as with Jonah, will yield true repentance. Notice He said the punishment is administered **by the Lord.** So once again the Lord has put His Church into a position where She will be uncomfortable unless She returns to righteousness.

Jonah was terribly uncomfortable in the belly of that whale, but God is more concerned with our *condition* than our *comfort*. Often if I am unable to wake my children, I will set them upright, making it uncomfortable for them to sleep. Could it be God is trying to rouse us?

Now let's look at Hosea 6:1-2 (NKJV) again: "Come and let us return to the Lord; for He has torn, but He will heal us; He has stricken, but He will bind us up. After **two days** He will revive us; on the third day He will raise us up, that we may live in His sight." [Emp. added]

What does Hosea mean, "**After two days**"? II Peter 3:8 says, ". . . with the Lord one day is as a thousand years, . . ."

so, literally, He is saying **after two thousand years** (the age of the Church now) He will revive us. First He will judge and refine, then He will heal and revive.

The third day (or thousand years) is the millennial reign of Christ. He will reign one thousand years here on earth in our sight. So we are living currently in the season of this prophecy's fulfillment. Let's keep reading.

"Let us know, let us **pursue** the knowledge of the Lord" (Hosea 6:3, NKJV).

What is our pursuit to be? Success, ministry, a good marriage, the blessings of God, healing, prosperity? God forbid! Our pursuit is to know Him! Saul pursued a kingdom; David pursued God. When you pursue Him—not for what He has or can do, but for who He is—you will find the treasures hidden with Him. It is in this secret place that gifts are given freely, never to be taken from you. Saul lost his kingdom while trying to hold on to it. Yet, because God had established David's kingdom, even when David yielded it to Absalom, God gave it back!

Keep in mind, before Jesus comes for His Church in rapture, He first will come in judgment, which will result in refining and, ultimately, revival.

> . . . Let us pursue the knowledge of the Lord. His **going forth is established** as the morning; He will come **to us** like the **rain**, like **latter and former rain** to the earth.
> [Emp. added]   Hosea 6:3 (NKJV)

Notice His coming ("going forth") is established. In other words, just as surely as the sun rises each morning at a **set or established time**, so, His coming in judgment, refining, and revival is set. He will come to the Church whether She is ready or not. He will come **suddenly**, as the rain—the **former and latter**. The **former rain** began with the days of John the Baptist. "For all the prophets and the law prophesied **until** John" (Matthew 11:13, NKJV). John the Baptist came warning of coming judgment, producing refining and revival. Those who didn't listen to John's warning and continued to mishandle God's people and offerings were **judged**. Jesus came to the temple and threw them out. He turned over their tables (symbolic of their system or structure) and threw out the money. This confrontation of the powerless *religious organization* of that day paved the way for a new form of worship. Jesus aggressively ministered to the needs of the masses, while opposing the religious Pharisees and their hypocrisy. We now stand at the threshold of just such a separation, as the Son of God exposes the hypocrisy of our own hearts and implants His compassion for the people.

> Therefore be patient, brethren, until the coming of the Lord. See how the farmer (the Father) waits for the precious fruit of the earth (His people), waiting patiently for it until it receives the **early and latter rain**. [Emp. added]   James 5:7 (NKJV)

We are on the verge of this latter rain. Once again, God is raising up prophets to warn His people of pending judgment. After this refinement and purging of the Church will come the revival of the outpouring of His Spirit. This outpouring will dwarf the outpouring in the book of Acts, for God said: "Be glad then, ye children of Zion, and rejoice in the Lord your God; for He hath given you the **former rain moderately**, and He will cause to come down for you the rain, the **former rain** and the **latter rain** in the first (month)" [Emp. added] (Joel 2:23). God says the former rain is **moderate** compared to the latter! Wow! In other words, what you see in the book of Acts is moderate compared with what we are about to enter. God always saves His best wine for last.

Ecclesiastes 7:8 says, "Better is the end of a thing than the beginning thereof . . ." God, through the prophet Haggai, says, "The **glory of this latter house** shall be **greater than of the former** [house], . . . and in this place will I give peace, . . ." [Emp. added] (Haggai 2:9). He spoke of the temple that was rebuilt after Israel's captivity. However, it has prophetic application also. The glory of God in His latter Church shall be greater than that of the former Church.

Some say, "We're in revival now." We are not in revival. We are in a mess. We are like the valley of dry bones Ezekiel saw. But herein lies our hope: God said to Ezekiel, ". . . Son of man, can these bones live? And I answered, O Lord GOD, thou knowest" (Ezekiel 37:3). The answer was, "YES!" Again He said to Ezekiel, ". . . **Prophesy** upon these bones, and say unto them, O ye dry bones, hear **the word of the LORD**. Thus saith the Lord GOD unto these bones; Behold, I will cause breath to enter into you, and **ye shall live:** . . . So I **prophesied** as He commanded me, and **the breath came into them, and they lived, and stood up upon their feet, an exceeding great army**" [Emp. added] (Ezekiel 37:4-5,10). God is getting ready to release His life and His breath into the lifeless body of the Church. Yes! This Church shall arise once again; its people will stand on their feet a glorious, victorious army, dead to their own lives but empowered by God's life.

Our condition—like a valley of dry bones—awaits His prophetic word to revive us. When we enter this revival, we won't need to be told. No one will be needed to point it out. It will be so evident that people will say, "But **this is that** which was spoken by the prophet Joel; . . ." [Emp. added] (Acts 2:16).

The Lord will come to His temple, first to judge and to refine, and then to revive before He catches us away in the twinkling of an eye. Now that we understand that God brings His Church into the wilderness to judge and refine it, let us see *how* He will do it.

CHAPTER 8

THE REFINING FIRE

God is raising a generation of people who will manifest His glory, not their own . . .

Behold, I send My messenger, And he will prepare the way before Me. And the Lord, whom you seek, will suddenly come to His temple, Even the Messenger of the covenant, In whom you delight. Behold, He is coming, says the LORD of hosts. But who can endure the day of His coming? And who can stand when He appears? For He [is] like a refiner's fire, And like fullers' soap. He will sit as a refiner and a purifier of silver; He will purify the sons of Levi, And purge them as gold and silver, That they may offer to the LORD An offering in righteousness.

Malachi 3:1-3 (NKJV)

God is raising a generation of people who will manifest *His* glory, not their own—a people made in His image, walking in His character.

> But in a great house there are not only
> **vessels** of **gold and of silver**, but also of
> **wood and of earth**; and some to **honour**,
> and some to **dishonour**. If a man therefore
> **purge** himself from these [iniquities], he
> shall be a vessel unto honour, sanctified, and
> meet for the master's use, [and] prepared
> unto every good work. [Emp. added]
>   II Timothy 2:20-21

Notice there are two types of vessels, both honorable and
dishonorable. The Greek word for dishonor, *atimia*, is defined
as dishonor, reproach, shame, **vile**. The Greek word for honor
is *time*, which is defined as **precious**. God says, "... If you take
out the **precious** from the **vile**, you shall be as My mouth"
[Emp. added] (Jeremiah 15:19, NKJV). How is the "precious"
taken from the "vile"? **Through purging** (see II Timothy 2:21,
above).The definition of **purge** is to cleanse thoroughly, or free
from impurities.

> He will sit as a **refiner** and a **purifier** of sil-
> ver; He will **purify the sons of Levi, and**
> *purge* **them as gold and silver**, that they may
> offer to the LORD an offering in righteous-
> ness. [Emp. added]   Malachi 3:3 (NKJV)

The "sons of Levi" are a foreshadowing of "the royal
priesthood" (I Peter 2:9), which is the Church. Since God
compares the refinement of this priesthood with the refinement process for gold and silver, it is important to understand the characteristics of gold and silver and how they
are refined. In this book we will discuss only gold, since the
refining process is similar for both silver and gold.

Gold has a beautiful yellow color, emitting a soft metal-
lic glow. It is widely distributed in nature but **always** in
small quantities, and **rarely is gold found in a pure state.**
In a pure state, gold is soft, pliable, and free from corrosion

or other substances. When gold is mixed with other metals (copper, iron, nickel, etc.) it becomes harder, less pliable, and more corrosive. This mixture is called an **alloy**. The higher the percentage of copper, iron, nickel, etc., the harder the gold becomes. Conversely, the lower the percentage of alloy, the softer and more flexible it is.

Immediately we see **the parallel: a pure heart** before God is like **pure gold**. A pure heart is soft, tender, and pliable.

> Therefore, as the Holy Spirit says: TODAY, if you will hear His voice, do not **harden** your **hearts** as in the rebellion, ... but exhort one another daily, while it is called "TODAY," lest any of you be **hardened through the deceitfulness of sin**. [Emp. added]
>
> Hebrews 3:7-13 (NKJV)

Sin is the added substance that turns our *pure* gold into an alloy, hardening our hearts. This lack of tenderness creates a loss of sensitivity, which hinders our ability to hear His voice. Unfortunately, this is the state of **many in the Church**, having a form of godliness, but without a tender heart. Their hearts no longer burn for Jesus. That white-hot love for God has been replaced with a frigid self love, which seeks only its own pleasure, comfort, and benefit. Supposing godliness is a means to personal gain (I Timothy 6:5), they seek only the benefits of the promise and exclude the Promisor Himself. DECEIVED, they delight themselves with the world, expecting to receive heaven, too!

> **Pure** and **undefiled** religion before God and the Father is this: ... **to keep oneself unspotted from the world**. [Emp. added]
>
> James 1:27 (NKJV)

Jesus is coming for a Church that is pure, without spot, or any such impurity (Ephesians 5:27), a Church Whose heart is unpolluted with the world's systems.

Another characteristic of gold is its resistance to rust or corrosion. Even though other metals tarnish as a result of atmospheric changes, changes in the atmosphere do not tarnish pure gold. Brass (a yellow alloy of copper and zinc), though it resembles gold, does not behave as gold. Brass tarnishes easily. It has gold's appearance without possessing its character. The higher the percentage of foreign substances in gold, the more susceptible it is to corrosion and corruption.

Presently, the world's system has leached into the Church. We have become **infiltrated** by its culture, and thus we are tarnishing. In America, the Church's values are polluted with worldliness. Many are insensitive and do not realize the need for purification.

Malachi 3:3 shows how Jesus will refine (or purge) His Church from the influence of the world, just as a refiner purifies gold. In the refining process, gold is ground into powder and then mixed with a substance called flux. The two are then placed in a furnace and melted by an intense **fire**. The **alloys** or impurities are drawn to the flux and rise to the surface. The gold (which is heavier) remains at the bottom. The impurities, or **dross** (such as copper, iron, and zinc, combined with flux), are then removed. Now examine how God refines:

> I will turn My hand against you, and thoroughly **purge** away your **dross**, and take away all your **alloy**. I will restore your judges [leaders] as at the first, and your counselors [Christians] as at the beginning. Afterward you shall be called the city of righteousness, the faithful city. [Emp. added]   Isaiah 1:25-26 (NKJV)

What is the fire He uses to refine us? The answer is found in the following passage:

> In this you greatly rejoice, though now

for a little while, **if need be,** you have been grieved [distressed] by various trials, that the **genuineness** of your faith, being much more precious than gold that perishes, **though it** [your faith] **is tested by fire,** may be found to praise, honor, and glory at the revelation of Jesus Christ. [Emp. added]

I Peter 1:6-7 (NKJV)

God's fire for refining is *trials and tribulations.* The heat of these separates our impurities from the character of God in our lives.

Another characteristic of gold, in its purest state, is its **transparency** (defined as the ability to see through, as glass). "And the street of the city [was] **pure gold,** like **transparent glass**" [Emp. added] (Revelation 21:21, NKJV). Once you are purified by the fiery trials, you become transparent! A transparent vessel brings no glory to itself, but it glorifies what it contains. It is unobstructive and almost unnoticeable. Once we are refined, the world again will see Jesus.

In Isaiah this is amplified to a greater degree:

Behold, I have refined you, but not as silver; I have tested you in the furnace of **affliction.** For My own sake, for My own sake, I will do it; For how should My name be profaned? [His name will no longer be dishonored because of sin and corruption among His own.] And I will not give My glory to another. [It will be His glory not the vessels'.] [Emp. added]   Isaiah 48:10-11 (NKJV)

The fire or furnace is **affliction,** not a literal physical fire, as that with which silver is refined, which explains why He says, "but not as silver." Our trials are the intense heat which separates the precious from the vile.

In December 1985, the Lord showed me He was going to

begin to purify my life. I got so excited, I told my wife, "God is going to remove my impurities." I proceeded to tell her all the undesirable things God would be removing. For the next three months, nothing happened. As a matter of fact, things got worse. I went to the Lord and asked, "Why are My bad habits getting worse, not better?" He responded, "Son, I said I was going to purify you. You have been trying to do it in your own strength. Now I will do it My way."

For years, people have tried to perfect holiness through their own ability. Denominations have been birthed as a result of our futile attempts to be pure. All we have done is enslave ourselves to the bondage of legalism. Holiness is a work of God's grace, not an outward restriction of the flesh. God gives grace to the humble, not the proud. The proud man thinks he can achieve holiness without God's help, by following rules and regulations. The humble man knows he can't and relies on the grace and strength of the Lord. So he pursues a relationship with God, knowing that only through a relationship will he be empowered to keep the laws written on his heart.

Again citing my own life as an example, as soon as God said He had begun the purification process, we started going through some very intense trials—trials such as I had never experienced before. And in the midst of them, God seemed so far away (**the wilderness**). Previously hidden personality flaws began to surface. I was rude and harsh with those closest to me. My family and friends avoided me.

I cried out to the Lord, "Where is all this anger coming from? It wasn't here before!" The Lord responded, "Son, when they purify gold they put it in fire and the fire causes it to become liquid. Then the impurities begin to show up at the surface." Then He asked me this question that changed my life. "Can you see the impurities in gold before it is put in the fire?" I said, "No." He said, "But that doesn't mean they're not there." He said, "When I put my fire under you, those impurities surfaced; though hidden to you, they were visible to me. So now the choice is yours; your reaction to what has been exposed will determine your future. You can remain angry and blame your wife, friends, pastor, or the people you work with for your condition, or you can see it for what it is and repent and ask forgiveness, and I'll take my ladle and remove those impurities from your life."

God does not remove them against our will. That is why Paul said in II Timothy 2:21, ". . . **cleanses himself.**" If you want to justify (i.e., make excuses for) and keep the flaws that hold you back, God will not force you to release them. Purification is a constant, ongoing, and often painful process, but, knowing its yield, I welcome it. Jesus says, "Blessed are the pure in heart, for they shall see God" (Matthew 5:8). David, who had a heart after God, cried out, "Who can understand his errors? Cleanse me from secret faults" (Psalm 19:12).

We read in Proverb 25:3, "The heaven for height, and the earth for depth, and the heart of kings [is] unsearchable." Don't just think "kings of nations" as you read this. He is talking about Christians. Revelation 1:6 says, "And hath made us **kings** and priests unto God and his Father; . . ." [Emp. added] Jesus has made us kings unto God and His Father. Also, God says in Proverb 25:3 that our hearts are unsearchable. But the previous verse says it is the glory of kings to search out a matter. How do we search our hearts if they are unsearchable? The answer: WE SEARCH OUR HEARTS through refining. For He goes on to say in the next two verses: "Take away the **dross** from the silver, and there shall come forth a vessel for the finer. Take away the **wicked** from before the **king,** and his throne shall be **established in righteousness**" [Emp. added] (Proverb 25:4-5).

The heart is unsearchable; however, God uses the fire of trials to cause what is hidden to be revealed, just as hidden dross in gold or silver is revealed by the furnace. Jesus admonishes the Church, "I counsel you to buy from Me gold refined in the fire, . . . that you may be clothed, that the shame of your nakedness may not be **revealed** . . ." [Emp. added] (Revelation 3:18, NKJV).

Let this be our cry. If we ask God to purify our hearts, He will remove those impurities hidden from our eyes. God knows our innermost thoughts and intents, even though we don't.

Recognize this spiritual time and season. As fiery trials hit, don't become angry, but look for their purpose. Examine your heart and allow God to remove the precious from the vile. Remember, refinement strengthens that which is already good and cleanses or removes that which weakens or defiles. Welcome His refining that you might be a vessel of honor, able to manifest His Glory.

CHAPTER 9

REFINE OR DEVOUR

When a man builds apart from God . . . whether it is his life, home, or even a ministry—it will not endure.

But who can **endure the day** of His coming? And who can **stand** when He **appears**? For He is like a refiner's fire, . . . [Emp. added]   Malachi 3:2 (NKJV)

He is coming as a fire. "For our God is a consuming fire" (Hebrews 12:29). No willful sin can stand in the presence of God's glory, which is why He is taking such great pains to prepare His temple.

The same fire has two functions, depending on what it contacts. It either refines or devours, purifies or consumes. Malachi asks the question, "**Who can endure the day** of His coming? And **who can stand** when He appears?" Paul addresses this in I Corinthians 3:9-10 (NKJV): "For we are God's fellow workers; you are God's field, **you are God's building**. According to the grace of God which was given me, as a wise master builder I have laid the foundation, and another builds on it. **But let each one take heed how he builds on it.**"

We need to pay careful attention to how we build our lives! In scriptures, the building of a house symbolizes the building of our lives and ministry. We belong to God, for we are His building.

> . . . Christ Jesus, who was faithful to Him who appointed Him, as Moses also was faithful **in all His house**. For this One has been counted worthy of more glory than Moses, inasmuch as He who **built the house** has more honor than **the house**. For every house is built by someone, but He who built all things is God. [Emp. added]
> Hebrews 3:1-4 (NKJV)

Notice who builds the house—The Lord. It is neither us nor the strength of our flesh. Whatever God builds remains; what we build *will not*. "Unless **the Lord builds the House**, they labor in vain who build it; . . ." [Emp. added] (Psalm 127:1, NKJV). When man builds apart from God—whether it is his life, home, or even a ministry—it will not endure.

In Genesis 11:4 (NKJV), we see an example of this: "Come, let us **build ourselves** a city, and a tower whose top is in the heavens; let us **make a name for ourselves** . . ." [Emp. added]

What was their motive?—to achieve their dreams; to raise their edifice for their own glory. They wanted to be as God, but totally independent of Him. The pursuit fulfilled their desires and their wills, not God's. They built apart from God even though it was a heavenly goal. This shows that no matter how noble our intent, without God it is an exercise in futility. This is why we are warned:

> . . . But let each one **take heed** how he builds on it. . . . Now if anyone builds on this foundation [which is Christ Jesus] with **gold, silver, precious stones, wood, hay,**

> **straw**, each one's **work** will become clear;
> for **the Day** ["who can endure **the day** of His
> coming?"] will declare it, because it will be
> revealed by fire; and **the fire will test** each
> one's work, of what sort it is. [Emp. added]
>   I Corinthians 3:10-13 (NKJV)

Gold, silver, and precious stones represent construction
God's way. Wood, hay, and straw represent our own methods of construction, by the blueprint of the world. Is this
verse talking only about judgment in heaven? No! It
describes when He **comes** to His temple (see verses 16-17).
He will come as fire. What does fire do? As we saw before,
it depends on what it contacts; the same fire that *consumes*
wood, hay, and straw *refines* gold and silver. That is why He
goes on to say, "If any man's work is burned, he will suffer
loss; but he himself will be saved, yet so as through fire"
(verse 15).

If you build your life, business, or ministry with bricks of
your own making, such as the strength of your personality, or
by worldly programs or techniques . . . if you build by manip-
ulating or controlling people through intimidation . . . if you
flatter and ride the coattails of others to gain position . . . if to
build, you tear down others through criticism or gossip . . .
then everything gained by these methods will be lost.
Whatever you have built shall be burned. Many promote
themselves, lying to gain advantage. This, too, will be
burned! "Let no one **deceive** himself. If anyone among you
seems to be wise in this age, let him **become a fool that he
may become wise**. For the wisdom of this world is foolish-
ness with God . . ." [Emp. added] (verses 18-19).

The focus of this world's wisdom is self. "But if you have
bitter **envy** and **self-seeking** in your hearts . . . This wisdom
does not descend from above, but is earthly, sensual, demon-
ic" [Emp. added] (James 3:14-15, NKJV). In God's eyes, any
area of your life where your motive is self-seeking is counted
as wood, hay, or straw. Regardless of how much it appears to

help others or operates in the name of the Lord, or of the amount of time that is sacrificed . . . it all burns. Envy begets competition and suspicion. Suspicion presently runs rampant in the Church, and the fear it brings causes division. We begin to "power position" ourselves in order to keep our domain safe. This posturing may cost us friends, integrity, or most importantly, our relationship with God. Often, even ministers are driven by the concerns of position, title, or salary, at the expense of God's heart. The weight of these chokes their love for God's people, and their ministries becomes self-serving. This causes the whole emphasis of their ministries to become performance based . . . striving to be the "best or biggest," hoping that this success will fill the void that, in fact, can be filled only by God. Deceived, they truly believe they are performing for God's sake.

Others, however, are seeking God's heart. The more they seek Him, the more they appear to decrease. They cry, "God, the more I seek you, the more I go down, not up." But God answers, "Dig deeper."

> Whoever **comes to Me**, and **hears** my sayings and **does** them, I will show you whom he is like: he is like a man **building a house**, who **dug deep** and laid the foundation on the rock. . . . [Emp. added]
> Luke 6:47-48 (NKJV)

When I lived in Dallas, I would watch builders erect skyscrapers. At first the progress was slow, while they spent months breaking rock and digging for the foundation. The bigger the building, the deeper and more extensive its foundation. From the ground above, it seemed they were moving slowly and making little headway; then all of a sudden, up it would go. Its progress would seem to occur almost overnight when compared with the preparation process. The *upward progression* was nothing when compared with the *downward preparation*.

There are many in the body of Christ in the process of downward preparation—and we praise God for the beginning of an awakening. They may have a call to ministry but are presently in a serving position. Things don't appear to be moving very quickly. . . . They are in the wilderness under God's preparation. The foundation is being laid; the character of Christ being formed. This character will undergird all who build for the ministry. Others around them appear to move swiftly upward through politics and self-promotion, while their own progress seems to remain at a standstill. They even may be tempted to take this route themselves, but knowing it yields no character and compromises the existing character they already have attained, they decide the risk is too great. By **waiting** on God, they allow the Master Builder to lay a good solid foundation on the Rock.

Presently, there are ministers diligently seeking God, but again it appears nothing is happening. They have found themselves in a **dry place or time**. They watch as others promote themselves and their ministries successfully through the use of programs and secular marketing. Yet God will not allow them to build through these methods. Why? Because God Himself is preparing their foundation.

Then there are those whom God has not called to full-time ministry as yet, but He has given them a dream. They are wondering how this vision will ever come to pass. Its possible fulfillment may appear to be slipping away.

In this dry or wilderness time, God separates those who will wait on Him from these who will build with the tools of "hype" or "programs." Promotion will come to those who are watching and waiting for Him to come to His temple.

God says, "When I choose the **[proper] time**, I will judge uprightly. . . . **for exaltation** comes neither from the east nor from the west nor from the south. But God is the Judge: He puts down one, and exalts another" [Emp. added] (Psalm 75:2-7, NKJV).

There are Isaac ministries and there are Ishmael ministries. What is the difference? Ishmael ministries are born of a need, but birthed by flesh; Isaac ministries are born of a call and birthed by Spirit. **Both come from the same promise or call of God.**

Let me explain: God promised Abram he would have a son. This son was to come from Abram's own body. God did not say anything about his barren wife Sarai's role in the matter. After **eleven years** of waiting, Sarai came to Abram with this idea: "I'm barren and past child-bearing age. Your reproductive system is still good. If we wait much longer, even you will be unable to reproduce. Don't you know? Faith without works is dead! So take my maid Hagar and get her pregnant, so I shall obtain my children from her" (paraphrased, Genesis 16). He listened to his wife's voice and Hagar gave him a son named **Ishmael**.

Now, God saw this and said, "So they think they can bring forth My promise in their own strength; now I will wait until Abram's reproductive system is dead. Then I'll bring forth My promise" (paraphrased). Why? Because no flesh will glory **in God's sight!** So thirteen years later, twenty-four years after the promise was made (and we get upset if our prayers aren't answered in two weeks!), God said, "Now that Abraham's reproductive system is dead (Romans 4:19), since he is about a hundred years old, I can now bring forth My promise." God revived both of their reproductive systems, and Sarah conceived and gave birth to Isaac. Ishmael was around the house for thirteen years before Isaac was born and a few more after, enjoying the benefits of the household of Abraham while Isaac was a child. But the day came when Ishmael began to persecute Isaac. Look what happened:

> . . . he who was **born according to the flesh** then persecuted him who was **born according to the Spirit, even so it is now.**

> Nevertheless what does the Scripture say?
> **Cast out** the bondwoman [Hagar] and her
> son [Ishmael], for the son of the bondwom-
> an shall **not be heir** with the son of the free-
> woman. [Emp. added]
>
> Galatians 4:29-30 (NKJV)

That born of flesh and need will **always** persecute what is born of the Spirit. Even now there are *Ishmael* ministries, ministries formed of flesh and need as a result of **a genuine promise**. Only they did not wait on God to bring it to pass; they brought it forth themselves.

This applies to all walks of life, not just ministries. Remember . . . **flesh can never bring forth God's promises!** If it is birthed by the flesh, flesh will have to provide for it. This usually will create an enviroment of manipulation and control. Those involved will power position themselves or play on human emotions to get results. All of the sudden **you** have become responsible for *their* success or failure, depending upon your response. There will be a lot of pressure and legalism involved. Even though we are addressing ministry practices, I want to emphasize that this is *not* just ministries I'm describing; this applies to *anything* created in the power of the flesh.

Conversely, that born of the Spirit will know it had no role in its own formation, so it knows it cannot maintain or cause growth in its own ability. The pressure will be on God to provide for what He created (or built).

When Isaac came forth, Ishmael's position was already well established. Historically, I have found that the opportunity for an Ishmael ministry will always present itself **before** the promised Isaac ministry is birthed. The temptation to bring forth yourself what God alone can provide must be resisted. Recall again the scripture, "**Cast out** the bondwoman and her son, for the son of the bondwoman shall **not be heir** with the son of the freewoman."

The day is coming when the Lord shall come to His temple and say, "Cast out the ministries of flesh, for the ministries of flesh shall have no inheritance with the ministries of promise." Even though they are producing fruit, God will say, "Cast them out!" Why? So that no flesh will glory in His presence!

When judgment comes, with its separation, if one portion of your life or ministry has been built by your own ability and the other by the Spirit, only the portion built by the Spirit of the Lord will remain. If an individual builds his ministry or life totally by self-promotion, then nothing shall remain. But he shall be saved, yet as through fire. The only things that will remain are those which are received by promise and conceived and birthed through the Holy Spirit.

CHAPTER 10

JUDGMENT OF THE WICKED

"Impostor": one who deceives others by an assumed character or false pretenses.

But who can endure the day of His coming? And who can stand when He appears? For He is like a refiner's fire and like launderer's soap. **He will sit as a refiner** and a purifier of silver; He will purify the sons of Levi, and purge them as gold and silver, that they may offer to the Lord an offering in righteousness.

Then the offering of Judah and Jerusalem will be pleasant to the Lord, as in the days of old, as in former years.

And I will come near you for judgment; I will be a swift witness against sorcerers, against adulterers, against perjurers, against those who exploit wage earners and widows and orphans, and against those who turn away an alien—because **they do not fear Me,** says the Lord of hosts. [Emp. added]

Malachi 3:2-5 (NKJV)

Malachi did not have access to New Testament terminology, so he used terms such as "sons of Levi" and "Judah and Jerusalem." In speaking prophetically to our day, he had to use his day's vocabulary.

Notice what God said He will do once His own children are refined. "I will come **near you** for judgment"; The key words are "near you." To clarify what He is saying we must understand that the wicked men or women against whom He is going to be a swift witness in judgment are *"near or among"* His people! In Jeremiah 5:26,28,29 (NKJV), another scripture which almost parallels Malachi, we find:

> For **among** my people are found wicked men; they lie in wait as one who sets snares; they set a trap; they catch men. . . . They have grown fat, they are sleek; yes, they surpass the deeds of the wicked; they do not plead the cause, the cause of the fatherless; yet they prosper, and the right of the needy they do not defend. Shall I not punish them for these things? says the Lord. Shall I not avenge Myself on such a nation as this? [Emp. added]

And two New Testament references:

> Therefore take heed to yourselves and to all the flock, among which the Holy Spirit has made you overseers, to shepherd the church of God which He purchased with His own blood. For I know this, that after my departure savage wolves will come in among you, not sparing the flock. Also from **among** yourselves men will rise up, speaking perverse things, to draw away the disciples after themselves. [Emp. added]
>
> Acts 20:28-30 (NKJV)

Yes, and all those who desire to live godly
in Christ Jesus will suffer persecution. But
evil men and **impostors** will grow worse
and worse, **deceiving** and **being deceived.**
[Emp. added]   II Timothy 3:12-13 (NKJV)

The wicked near or among God's people are called
impostors. The dictionary defines the word "impostor" as
one who deceives others by an assumed character or false
pretenses. In order to understand, we must realize:

. . . The kingdom of heaven is like a man
[Jesus] who sowed good seed [sons of the
kingdom] in his field; But while men slept
[the Church not watching and praying], his
enemy [the devil] came and sowed tares
[wicked men who appear as Christians]
among the wheat [those who are truly His]
and went his way. [Emp. added]
Matthew 13:24-25 (NKJV)

Notice the tares were sown **among** the wheat. A tare
looks like wheat . . . *until* harvest time, that is. Then the difference becomes evident, the wheat will have **fruit** while
the tares have none.

Not all who claim to know Jesus, actually know Him.
Now, it is not my intention to breed suspicion, but to
reemphasize what is already described clearly in scripture. Jesus warned us, "Beware of false prophets, who
come to **you in sheep's clothing,** but inwardly they are
ravenous wolves. Disguised as sheep their *appearance* is
similar but their *fruit* is not" [Emp. added] (Matthew 7:15-
20, NKJV). We must develop the discernment to recognize
"good" or "bad" fruit.

The book of Jude covers this in detail. "For certain men
have **crept in unnoticed,** who long ago were marked out
for this condemnation, ungodly men, who turn the grace of

our God into licentiousness and **deny the only Lord God and our Lord Jesus Christ**" [Emp. added] (Jude 4, NKJV).

You may be thinking to yourself that there is no way your church has any in attendance who deny the Lord. Well, it is important that you understand *how* they deny Him. Notice the scripture says "crept in unnoticed." It is not by what they *say*, but in what they do (how they live, etc.) that they deny Him. To clarify this, look at what Titus said: "They profess [confess] to know God, but in **works they deny Him**, . . ." [Emp. added] (Titus 1:16, NKJV). So the only way to discern them is by their fruits, not their words! Jude goes on to say: "But I want to remind you, though you once knew this, that the Lord, having saved the people out of Egypt, afterward destroyed those who did not believe" (Jude 5). He parallels the false sheep of today with the false ones in the wilderness who fell under the judgment of God. With some, the earth opened up and swallowed them alive (Numbers 16:31-32). Many died by the plague before the Lord (Numbers 14:37; 25:9). Others died of serpent bites (Numbers 21:6). And in New Testament and present times:

> Likewise also these dreamers defile the flesh, reject authority, and speak evil of dignitaries. . . . Woe to them! For they have gone in the way of Cain, have run greedily in the error of Balaam for profit, and perished in the rebellion of Korah.   Jude 8,11 (NKJV)

Cain, Balaam, and Korah **were at one time in fellowship with or in the service of God.** Cain was jealous of his brother, whose offering (the best of his flock) was accepted by God, while Cain's offering (the fruit of his hands) was rejected. He became offended, even after God instructed Him that if he would do right he would be accepted. It was easier for him to remain angry and offended at his brother than to deal with the iniquity in his heart. This offense turned to hatred, which eventually manifested itself as murder. "Whoever hates his brother is a murderer, and you know that no murderer has eternal life abiding in him" (I John 3:15, NKJV).

Balaam was greedy for power, position, and money. He prostituted the anointing on his life in the hope of gaining riches, even after God specifically instructed him not to do so. "But those who desire to be rich fall into temptation and a snare, and into many foolish and harmful lusts which drown men in destruction and perdition" (I Timothy 6:9, NKJV). Because of this, Balaam died among the Canaanites when Israel came to possess the land.

Korah was a priest, a descendant of Levi, yet he rose up against Moses and Aaron in the wilderness, saying, "You take too much upon yourselves, . . . why then do you exalt yourselves above the assembly of the Lord?" (Numbers 16:3, NKJV). He was not concerned that Moses had too big a load, he just wanted some of the authority Moses had. His hidden agenda was to promote himself. Insubordinate to God's appointed leadership, he accused Moses (whom God had exalted) of exalting himself. Korah's rebellion was judged, and he was swallowed alive by the earth. The New Testament says: "Obey those who rule over you, and be submissive, for they watch out for your souls, as those who must give account. Let them do so with joy and not with grief, for that would be unprofitable for you" (Hebrews 13:17, NKJV).

In summation, Cain, Balaam, and Korah were unable to maintain their relationship with God because their goals were only to **serve themselves**, not God or His people. Jude goes on to say: "These are **spots** in your **love feasts**, while they feast with you without fear, **serving only themselves** . . ." [Emp. added] (Jude 12, NKJV). Love feasts are church services. Jude describes them as "spots." Jesus is coming back for a "glorious church, not having **spot** or wrinkle or any such thing" [Emp. added] (Ephesians 5:27, NKJV). This means these men and women will be purged from the Church, unless they repent prior to His return.

Jude continues: "They are clouds without water, carried about by the winds; . . ." Clouds without water describes their condition of having the appearance of godliness, but being void of life or substance and yielding no rain.

Then Jude says: "They are . . . late autumn trees **without fruit, twice dead,** pulled up by the roots; raging waves of the sea, foaming up their own shame; wandering stars for whom is reserved the blackness of darkness forever" [Emp. added] (Jude 12-13, NKJV).

Notice he says "**twice dead.**" To be twice dead means you were once dead without Christ, then you were made alive by receiving Him, then you died again by departing from Him permanently. Peter confirms this in chapter two of his second book:

> . . . They are **spots** and blemishes, carousing in their own deceptions while **they feast with you,** having eyes full of adultery and that cannot cease from sin, enticing unstable souls. **They have a heart trained in covetous practices,** and are accursed children. **They have forsaken the right way and gone astray,** . . . For if, after they have escaped the pollutions of the world through the knowledge of the Lord and Savior Jesus Christ, they are again entangled in them and overcome, the latter end is worse for them than the beginning. For it would have been better for them not to have known the way of righteousness, than **having known it, to turn** from the holy commandment delivered to them. [Emp. added]
> II Peter 2:13-15, 20-21 (NKJV)

I have used a lot of scripture in this chapter. With such a

volatile issue, I felt it was important to use predominantly scriptures, rather than my own opinion or convictions. Let me call your attention to three specific facts:

1. These impostors are **among** God's people.
2. These are men and women who once knew the way of righteousness but have forsaken it permanently.
3. They have a form of godliness, but their motive is only self-serving.

Their god is their belly and they glory in their shame. Their hearts are trained in covetous practices.

How can we recognize them? By judging their fruits! Now, just because a man sins, he is not necessarily an impostor. King David committed adultery with a woman and murdered her husband. But when confronted by the prophet Nathan, David fell on his face and repented. The Bible says that King David was a man after God's heart. Obviously, God saw that David brought forth fruit worthy of repentance and judged his heart, not his actions.

King Saul, on the other hand, *only* spared a few sheep, oxen, and the king of Amelek. When he was confronted by the prophet Samuel he said, "I have sinned; yet honor me now, please, before the elders of my people and before Israel, . . ." (I Samuel 15:30, NKJV).

Saul seemed unaware that he had sinned against God; he wanted to be sure this mishap wouldn't change his position in the eyes of his elders or the people. He was totally unconcerned about his relationship with God. He was serving only his own interests.

If we graded **only** the visible manifestation of the sins of both men, we would classify David as a wicked man and Saul as a man who missed it. But judging only by outward standards, we would be wrong! God rejected Saul but established David's kingdom. God does not view actions (those things visible to man), but our hearts.

Fruit is a product or outflow of the heart. No man can

know another's heart—we scarcely know our own—but we are able to recognize fruit. A man may try to befriend you outwardly, yet inwardly his motive is to take advantage of you. The whole key is the heart motive, which we find manifested in the wilderness.

Again, a word of caution. Discernment is not **suspicion**. Suspicion is fear-motivated (i.e., what will happen or how will this affect me?). Fear is not from God, so this type of "discernment" is usually incorrect. Proper discernment will be a result of concern for others and their welfare. It will not carry with it a hidden agenda or critical spirit. "And this I pray, that your **love may abound** still more and more in knowledge and **all discernment**" [Emp. added] (Philippians 1:9, NKJV). Perfected love casts out fear and gives an atmosphere where discernment, not suspicion, can flow.

Jesus discerned and confronted the wickedness and hypocrisy of the Pharisees, yet He loved them enough to die for them. Even so, if you properly discern, you will pray rather than gossip. God even may lead you to go to that person. Again, a good check for this leading is your motive. Is it to let them know how spiritual you are? Or to let them know you are upset? Or is it to go to them for restoration or correction so others won't be hurt . . . or pray for wisdom for those in authority that they may discern properly? Paul said, "Finally, brethren, pray for us, . . . that we may be delivered from unreasonable and wicked men; . . ." (II Thessalonians 3:1-2, NKJV).

Now let's review Malachi. The Lord first will send His messenger, the prophetic anointing, to *warn* and call God's people to repentance. Then He will come to His temple to *refine* those who received the prophetic word, that they might worship Him acceptably. Then He will *judge* swiftly the wicked among His own that rejected His warning by the prophetic word or anointing.

First, God issues a warning, then He works refinement, and last He executes judgment. I believe the warning is now being sounded, working refinement in the hearts of those who receive it. It is important to note that prophets don't bring judgment, they warn of it; the prophetic is not to be feared, but heeded.

We see this pattern clearly in the gospels. John the Baptist came preaching a baptism of repentance and warning the people of pending judgment.

> But when he [John the Baptist] saw many of the Pharisees and Sadducees coming to his baptism, he said to them, Brood of vipers! Who has warned you to flee from the wrath [**or judgment**] to come? Therefore **bear fruits** worthy of **repentance**, and do not think to say to yourselves, We have Abraham as our father. For I say to you that God is able to raise up children to Abraham from these stones. And even now the ax is laid to the root of the trees. Therefore every tree which does **not bear good fruit** is cut down and thrown into **the fire.** I indeed baptize you with water unto repentance, but He who is coming after me is mightier than I, whose sandals I am not worthy to carry. He will baptize you with the Holy Spirit **and fire.** His winnowing fan is in His hand, and He will thoroughly clean out His threshing floor, and gather His **wheat** [those who are truly His] into the barn; but He will **burn up the chaff** with **unquenchable fire.** [Emp. added]   Matthew 3:7-12 (NKJV)

John *warned* that judgment would come if there were no true repentance. He said *true* repentance would bring forth *good* fruit, and *no* repentance would bring forth *no* change. If there were no true repentance, the ax would be put to the root, which is the life source of the fruit—**the heart.** This ax would cut down the tree from His vineyard. Jesus warned:

> I tell you, no; but unless you repent you
> will all likewise perish. He also spoke this
> parable: A certain man had a fig tree planted
> in his vineyard, and he came seeking fruit
> on it and **found none** [no repentance]. Then
> he said to the keeper of his vineyard, Look,
> for three years I have come seeking fruit on
> this fig tree and find none. **Cut it down;** why
> does it use up the ground? But he answered
> and said to him, Sir, let it alone this year also,
> until I dig around it and fertilize it. And **if it
> bears fruit, well. But if not, after that you
> can cut it down.** [Emp. added]
>
> Luke 13:5-9 (NKJV)

John the Baptist was one who dug around the trees and
fertilized them. He broke up the fallow ground, softening it
to receive the coming refinement. He loved the people
enough to warn them and tell them the truth. John was
great in the sight of God (Luke 1:15). It is one thing to be
great in the sight of men, but quite another to be great in
God's sight.

Because John feared the rejection of God more than the
rejection of man, he was able to tell the truth. A false witness flatters; a true witness speaks the truth, even at the risk
of being rejected.

Then John gave a second example. He told how Jesus
had His winnowing fan in His hand, and that He would
thoroughly clean out His **threshing floor**. The point I want
to make is *Jesus* will **thoroughly** clean His temple. There is
nothing hidden from Him. This is why Jesus was able to
look at those Jews and say, "... But unless you repent you
will all likewise perish."

Oh, people! There must be a change in the Church! Too
often our motives are wrong. We say we are doing something for the Lord, when really we are doing it to benefit
our own hidden agenda. The Church rarely intercedes ...

sighing and crying over the abominations within. Our senses are dulled while the enemy continues to eat and devour. We think we are rich and have need of nothing, when in actuality we are blind to our true state and condition (Revelation 3:15-17). Even now God is bringing His warning and refining process. Change must come to the Church; indeed, it will come! It must begin with leadership, not only inside the walls of the church but in the homes. It must happen with the fathers. There must be a revolution in the way we think and live. Our fathers' and leaders' hearts must be turned back to the children and people.

God exposes the wicked and the impostors among His people. He will judge them—not the prophets! John the Baptist warned of judgment; Jesus refined the temple by cleansing it; and much later, *God* destroyed the temple in judgment.

CHAPTER 11

INSTRUMENTS OF REFINING

It is character that makes a man of God, not anointing.

Wherein ye greatly rejoice, though now for a season, if need be, ye are in **heaviness** through manifold temptations: That the trial of your faith, being much more precious than of gold that perisheth, though **it be tried with fire**, might be found unto praise and honour and glory at the appearing of Jesus Christ: [Emp. added]   I Peter 1:6-7

Peter is describing how trials and temptations yield the refinement. The word **"heaviness"** is the Greek word *lupeo*. One of its definitions is **"to distress."** So we can say that during **times of stress** our hearts are refined.

But know this, that in the last days perilous times [**times of stress**] will come: for men will be lovers of themselves, lovers of money, boasters, proud, blasphemers, dis-

obedient to parents, unthankful, unholy,
unloving, unforgiving, slanderers, without
self-control, brutal, despisers of good,
traitors, headstrong, haughty, lovers of pleasure rather than lovers of God, **having a
form of godliness but denying its power.**
And from such people turn away! . . . Now
as Jannes and Jambres resisted Moses, so do
these also resist the truth: men of corrupt
minds, disapproved concerning the faith;
but they will progress no further, for their
folly will be manifest to all, as theirs also
was. But you have carefully followed my
doctrine, manner of life, purpose, faith,
longsuffering, love, perseverance, **persecutions, afflictions,** which happened to me at
Antioch, at Iconium, at Lystra—what persecutions I endured. And out of them all the
Lord delivered me. Yes, and all who desire
to **live godly** in Christ Jesus will **suffer persecution.** But **evil men** and **impostors** will
grow worse and worse, **deceiving and
being deceived.** [Emp. added]
                          II Timothy 3:1-5, 8-13 (NKJV)

Does this scripture sound like it is describing the state of
the world today? Of course! In fact, it reads like the daily
headlines. The sad thing is it also describes accurately the
condition of the Church. Notice in the beginning of these
verses that it says in the last days **"perilous times"** shall
come. These **times of stress** will result in part from impostors who have a **form of godliness, but no fruit.**

It is important to note that the anointing is not necessarily the sign of God's approval on a person's life. Paul
admonished Timothy to follow his (Paul's) manner of life.
Paul knew it would be the fruit in Timothy's life that would
carry the office and anointing God had commissioned to

his care. Notice even though God wrought miracles and healings at the hand of Paul, this was not what Paul felt was important for Timothy to observe and follow. He told Timothy to follow his example of *character*, which was validated by the fruit of the spirit. "But the fruit of the Spirit is love, joy, peace, longsuffering, gentleness, goodness, faith, meekness, temperance: against such there is no law" (Galatians 5:22-23).

One of the sources of stress will be the impostors who conduct themselves with life-styles described by II Timothy 3:2-4. The other source of stress will come from outside the Church, from evil men and the world's system. They (the impostors) will have a form of godliness and, as we say in religious circles, "only talk the talk"; some will even have supernatural signs following them. However, their hearts are not for the Lord, nor for His people, but rather for themselves and their own interests.

Notice right in the middle of this Paul says, "Yea, and all that will live godly in Christ Jesus shall suffer persecution." The persecution is part of the refining process. From whom will the persecution come? The impostors!—the ones who have infiltrated God's people. That is why Paul speaks of Jannes and Jambres resisting Moses. These were people in the congregation of the Lord, not outsiders.

Paul describes some of the persecutions and perils he faced in his ministry, and he tells us that some of the afflictions he encountered were from **"false brethren"** (II Corinthians 11:26).

This refining, though not limited to this, can come from someone who once walked with God and since has turned away from Him. He still may have the form of godliness and even "talk the talk," but his heart is for himself, not the Lord.

Look at what David cried out:

My heart is sore pained within me: and
the terrors of death are fallen upon me.
Fearfulness and trembling are come upon

me, and horror hath overwhelmed me. . . .
For [it was] **not an enemy [that] reproached
me;** then I could have borne [it]: neither
[was it] he that hated me [that] did magnify
[himself] against me; then I would have hid
myself from him: **But [it was] thou, a man
mine equal, my guide, and mine acquain-
tance. We took sweet counsel together,
[and] walked unto the house of God in
company.** . . . As for me, I will call upon
God; and the LORD shall save me. [Emp.
added]   Psalm 55:4-5, 12-14, 16

God chose David to be king. He was anointed before his
family and friends by the prophet Samuel. Encompassed
by God's favor, David went from shepherd boy to King
Saul's aide. David met Goliath on the battlefield, winning
both an overwhelming victory for Israel and King Saul's
daughter to be his wife. He was given a place of honor at
the king's table and a room at the palace. Jonathan, the
king's son, became his closest friend. David accompanied
Saul wherever he went in battle. It would seem his training
for the throne was almost complete. Everything he touched
prospered; he could do no wrong, *until* . . . the day the people began to compare him favorably with the King. Because
of the hand of God on his life, the women sang, "Saul has
slain his thousands, and David his ten thousands" (I
Samuel 18:7). Then King Saul's true nature came out,
expressed as anger and jealousy. He loved David as long as
David was an asset to *his* kingdom, but now he began to
view him as a threat. To protect his throne, he tried to kill
David. He threw spears at him and raised an army to find
and kill him. For sixteen years he chased David from cave
to cave in the wilderness. David must have thought,
"Where did I go wrong?" I'm sure he was hurt by Saul's
rejection. He must have loved and admired Saul, and now
God was using King Saul's madness to refine David.

You may be saying, "Saul was anointed by Samuel, too."
Yes, he was the Lord's anointed. However, the *anointing* is not
the *approval* of God. As a young man he started out humble in
his own sight. But as with many men who are unrefined or
unbroken, when success or power are given to them it will
reveal their true character. It is character that makes a man of
God, not the anointing. Men in scripture and throughout history have fallen as a result of attaining success without first
achieving the character to handle it. This character is the fruit
of the Spirit, and fruit is cultivated and gifts are given.
Cultivating or growing fruit takes time, but before you grow
anything, a seed must first go into the ground and die to
itself. On the other hand, gifts are not grown; they are given.
Gifts can be imparted in an instant. So do not be deceived.
Jesus said we would recognize a true man of God by his
fruits, not by his gifts. The approval of God on a person's life
is the *fruit* of the Spirit not the *gifts* of the Spirit.

The wilderness is where the man is refined and God's
character is developed whithin him. It is in this furnace of
affliction and persecution that the truly godly man is made.
Romans 5:3-4 (NKJV) says, ". . . we also glory [rejoice] in
tribulations, knowing that tribulation produces perseverance; and perseverance, [produces **approved**] **character**; and
character, hope." The approval of God on David's life was
because he was a man after the heart of God, not a man after a
kingdom! King Saul never went through a perfecting wilderness; therefore, he remained unbroken and insecure. David
did, however, and God used King Saul to send him there!

Another tool God wields to refine his servants takes the
form of carnal or immature fellow Christians or family members. Joseph's relationship with his brothers provides a classic
example of this:

> Now Israel [Jacob] loved Joseph more
> than all his children, because he was the son
> of his old age: and he made him a coat of
> many colours. And when his brethren saw

> that their father loved him more than all his
> brethren, they hated him, and could not
> speak peaceably unto him. And Joseph
> dreamed a dream, and he told it his breth-
> ren: and they hated him yet the more.
>
> Genesis 37:3-5

Joseph's brothers, who (with Joseph) were the fathers of
the twelve tribes of Israel, were jealous of their brother. In
Joseph's dream he saw his father, mother, and eleven brothers bowing down to him. He shared it with them, which
only fanned their hatred into a flame.

His brothers went to the fields to tend the flocks. After a
while Jacob sent Joseph to see how his brothers were doing.
"And when they saw him afar off, even before he came near
unto them, they conspired against him to slay him. And
they said one to another, Behold, this dreamer cometh.
Come now therefore, and let us slay him, and cast him into
some **pit**, and we will say, Some evil beast hath devoured
him: and **we shall see what will become of his dreams**"
[Emp. added] (Genesis 37:18-20).

They were envious of Joseph and tried to keep him from
successfully fulfilling the call of God on his life, without
realizing that they were becoming the instruments of God
to see the prophecy fulfilled. The Lord spoke this to me one
day and said, "Son, no man or devil can ever get you out of
my will as long as you obey Me. You are the only one who
can get yourself out of My will." **What these angry brothers meant for harm, God was going to use to fulfill the
dream!** So, as they were sitting down to eat after throwing
him into the pit (**PIT** stands for "Prophet In Training"),
they saw a company of Ishmaelites coming by on their way
to Egypt.

> And Judah said unto his brethren, What
> profit [is it] if we slay our brother, and con-
> ceal his blood? Come, and let us sell him to

> the Ishmaelites, and let not our hand be upon
> him; for he [is] our brother [and] our flesh.
> And his brethren were content. Then there
> passed by Midianites merchantmen; and
> they drew and lifted up Joseph out of the pit,
> and sold Joseph to the Ishmaelites for twenty
> [pieces] of silver: and they brought Joseph
> into Egypt.   Genesis 37:26-28

Joseph was taken to Egypt and sold to Potiphar, an officer of Pharaoh. Now he was a slave in another man's house. God began to prosper Joseph, and he won the favor of his master. Once his position was established in Potiphar's house, Potiphar's wife began to cast longing eyes toward Joseph. She wanted to sleep with him. But he refused, saying, "How can I do this great wickedness, and sin against God?" However, one day while alone with her in the house, she grabbed his garment and demanded that he lie with her. He ran out of the house, leaving his garment. Scorned, she told her husband he had tried to rape her. Then Potiphar took Joseph and put him in Pharaoh's prison. Joseph was protecting Potiphar's household. He had worked faithfully as a steward of Potiphar's house, causing it to prosper. It would appear that the more Joseph followed God, the worse his situation became. Indirectly, this was his brothers' fault; they had sent him to Egypt. Here was Joseph's wilderness. God's dream and Jacob's favor seemed so far away. This was a perfect opportunity for Joseph to become bitter. He could have spent his years in Egypt plotting revenge on his brothers. This spanned some fifteen to seventeen years. All natural hope was lost; how could this dream come to pass? But Joseph was in the process of preparation, becoming a vessel for the Lord. Others in situations not nearly as severe would say, "It is because of my pastor or my family or my friends or my mate that I am in this place of dryness. It is their fault I am not fulfilling God's call on my life."

But how did God describe Joseph's situation?

> **He** [God] sent a man before them, [even]
> Joseph, [who] was sold for a servant: Whose
> feet they hurt with fetters: he was laid in
> iron: **Until the time that his word came: the
> word of the LORD tried him.** [Emp. added]
> Psalm 105:17-19

The Lord said that He Himself was the one who sent
Joseph before his brothers. God used the anger of Joseph's
brothers to refine Joseph, to enable Joseph to fulfill the
dream and be the type of leader who would pull Egypt, as
well as his own family, through the famine it would face. It
was while Joseph was in prison and in pain that the word of
the Lord came to him.

This is a good place to point out an important fact: **you
don't have to look for the wilderness; God will lead you
there.** It is where you are tested (refined). Notice what the
scripture said in Psalm 105:19: "Until the time that his word
came: **the word of the LORD tried [or refined] him**" [Emp.
added].

God may have shown you dreams and visions of what
He has called you to do. He may have spoken to you of
the plans that He has for you. It often seems, however,
that the more you seek the Lord and obey His Word, the
further you get from the dream He has put in your heart.
You may have watched others be promoted in ministry
(or any other area of life), while you seem to be going in
the opposite direction of the dream God gave you. You
may be doing everything you know to do right. There
may be others around you who are carnal and not seeking the Lord, but they appear to be prospering, and they
are being promoted. They are the ones receiving the
financial and social "blessings." There may be people
who are being promoted by their own flattery or manipulation. There may be people who are doing things dis-

honestly, doing things by lying and cheating, yet still it appears they are "blessed," while you are in chains in Pharaoh's dungeon. What are you doing about it? Are you complaining? Look what God says about it.

> Your words have been harsh against Me, says the Lord, Yet you say, What have we spoken against You? You have said, It is useless to serve God; What profit is it that we have kept His ordinance, And that we have walked as mourners before the Lord of hosts? So now we call the proud blessed, For those who do wickedness are raised up; they even tempt God and go free.
> Malachi 3:13-15 (NKJV)

What are the complainers saying here? They're saying, "What profit is it that we've obeyed God, because we're going nowhere. It is the wicked, not us, who prosper." (This is the "Bevere Paraphrase.") God calls this harsh talk, and He views it as being directed against Him. More plainly put, it is murmuring and complaining.

God is finding out who is going to pursue Him and who is going to pursue the benefits. What some *call* blessings and what *really are* blessings are two different things. Some blessings may not last if your attitude (heart) is not right. Look what the Lord said He would do to those who are proud (and to their blessings):

> And now, O ye **priests**, this commandment is for you. If ye will not hear, and if ye will not lay it to heart, to give glory unto my name, saith the LORD of hosts, I will even send a curse upon you, and **I will curse your blessings**: yea, I have cursed them already, because ye do not lay it to heart. [Emp. added]   Malachi 2:1-2

Our inheritance does not consist of things or positions. Our inheritance is the Lord! Ezekiel 44:28 says, "And it shall be unto them [the priests who faithfully serve God] for an inheritance: **I am their inheritance**: and ye shall give them no possession in Israel: I am their possession" [Emp. added]. Many in the Church have gotten their eyes off of the *true* inheritance and instead on things or positions. These things or positions even may have been given by God. But it is like the son who is more interested in what his father gives him than in the fellowship of his father. I have three sons, and I love to give to them. However, it would break my heart if the only reason they gave me attention was to get from me what they wanted. Look at what Malachi goes on to say:

> Then they that feared the LORD spake
> **often** one to another: and the LORD hear-
> kened, and heard it, and a book of remem-
> brance was written before him for them that
> feared the LORD, and that thought upon his
> name. [Emp. added]   Malachi 3:16

These are the ones who are not seeking position, recognition, or "things." They seek the heart of God! The desire to *know* Him burns in them. You can talk to them about social things or business things, but their heart burns when you talk to them about the Lord or what He is saying. These are the ones about whom Luke said, "And they said one to another, Did not our heart burn within us, while he [Jesus] talked with us by the way, and while he opened to us the scriptures?" (Luke 24:32). Their desires are set on the things of the Spirit. They are saying, "I just want to know God; I want to please Him; I hunger and thirst for the word of the Lord; I want Him to take joy in me for He is the source of my joy." That's all that matters. **Their first love is Jesus, not the ministry.** They don't care whether they are in the middle of the desert or preaching to millions.

The difference between King Saul and King David now can be seen easily. Saul desired the throne; David desired the Lord! Both of them were tested. In the testing, the true motives of their hearts came out. When Absalom, David's son, conspired to take his father's throne, David's response was basically, "If God is through with me, then let Absalom have the throne, but if He is not through with me then God will put me back on it" (II Samuel 15:25, paraphrased). Now compare Saul's actions in similar circumstances. When Saul even suspected there would be a chance of David getting his throne, he wasted more than ten years trying to protect it by chasing the young man with an army of three thousand men. I use the term "wasted" because our efforts are futile if we use them to avoid the inevitable, namely, God's plan. Saul was after position, not the heart of God. He spent his life protecting his "blessings." The sad thing is that God, in fact, did put him on the throne, but Saul loved what was given to him more than the One who gave it to him.

Look again at what Malachi said, ". . . a book of remembrance was written before him for them that feared the LORD, and that thought upon his name." The Lord is searching for those whose hearts are loyal to Him, even in the dry times. As He finds them, He is recording them and their heart's cry in a book of remembrance. For what they desire shall be granted unto them. However, as stated earlier, the flesh or the counterfeit always comes first and will persecute the true. But while the true seem to be getting nowhere toward the promise, God says He is writing a book of remembrance of them because they have a divine appointment with God. It is called the Day that He comes to His temple to glorify it. Isaiah 60:7 says, ". . . and I will glorify the house of my glory."

Look at what Malachi goes on to say:

> For, behold, the day cometh, that shall **burn** as an oven; and all the **proud**, yea, and all that do **wickedly**, shall be **stubble**: and the

day that cometh shall burn them up, saith the
LORD of hosts, that it shall leave them neither
root nor branch [John cried out that the ax is
laid to the root of the trees that do not bear
fruit]. **But unto you that fear my name** [these
are the ones who often spoke to one another in
the dry times] **shall the Sun of righteousness
arise with healing in his wings** [Remember,
Hosea said, 'Come, and let us return to the
Lord; for He has torn, but **He will heal us**; He
has stricken, but He will bind us up.']; and ye
shall go forth, and grow up as calves of the
stall. And ye shall tread down the wicked; for
they shall be **ashes** under the soles of your feet
in the day that I shall do [this], saith the LORD
of hosts. [Emp. added]   Malachi 4:1-3

Look closely again at the last part of this scripture. God
says the one who fears the Lord shall arise and go forth and
tread down the wicked, for they (the wicked) shall be ashes
under the soles of the righteous' feet. There are two major
points at issue here that will pull everything together.

First, the **Sun** (not Son) of righteousness will **arise** in those
who have been refined. The "Sun of righteousness" speaks of
our God the "Consuming Fire!" Isaiah 60:1 says, "Arise,
shine; for thy light is come, and the **glory of the LORD** is
risen upon thee." The glory of the Lord is a consuming fire,
and it will devour any pride or wickedness that comes before
Him. Notice, it says the glory shall *arise* upon thee. Why *arise*?
II Corinthians 4:6-7 answers this: "For God, who commanded
the light to shine out of darkness, hath **shined** in our **hearts**,
to [give] the **light** of the knowledge of the **glory of God** in the
face of Jesus Christ. **But we have this treasure in earthen vessels**, that the excellency of the power may be of God, and not
of us" [Emp. added]. We have the glory of God in earthen
vessels! Why is the glory not manifested? The answer is
because the vessels are not yet refined. As we recall from our

previous chapter on refining, gold vessels that are refined by God are transparent. Malachi is saying in these two chapters that the Lord will come to His temple as a FIRE and will refine those who fear him. But once they are made pure, then the FIRE that refined them now will arise in them, since they are now transparent vessels, and consume the pride and wickedness around them.

Second, we must realize our warfare is not against flesh and blood, but against evil spirits. There are many who will see pride and wickedness in their own lives and will forsake it. However, there are those who will refuse to repent of their pride and wickedness. They love their sin, so when it is judged, they will be judged with it! **They have chosen their ways, not God's.** "There is a way which seemeth right unto a man, but the end thereof [are] the ways of death" [Emp. added] (Proverb 14:12). That is why the Lord is sending the prophets before He comes to judge to ". . . **prepare the way** . . ." He says the wicked shall be ashes under the soles of the righteous' feet! Ashes are the remains of something that has been consumed by FIRE!

Now look at Isaiah 4:3-6:

> And it shall come to pass, [that he that is] left in Zion, and [he that] remaineth in Jerusalem, shall be called **holy**, [even] every one that is written among the living in Jerusalem: When the Lord shall have washed away the filth of the daughters of Zion, and shall have **purged** the blood of Jerusalem from the midst thereof by the **spirit of judgment**, and by **the spirit of burning.** And the LORD will create upon every dwelling place of mount Zion, and upon her assemblies, **a cloud and smoke by day, and the shining of a flaming fire by night: for upon all the glory [shall be] a defence.** And there shall be a tabernacle for

a shadow in the daytime from the heat, and
for **a place of refuge,** and for a covert from
storm and from rain. [Emp. added]

That sums it up! Before the glory of the Lord is revealed
in the Church, the Lord will purge Her of the filth by the
spirit of judgment and the spirit of burning. Then She shall
be a place of refuge from the storms of evil in the world.

We see this with Joseph. Let's look one more time at
Psalm 105:19: "Until the time that his word came: the word
of the LORD tried [refined] him." Joseph was purified so
that he could be the **able vessel to bring forth what God
revealed in his dream** in the beginning. The Lord removed
all the impurities by the **spirit of burning.** Joseph was
released from prison by Pharaoh in one day, because he
interpreted Pharaoh's dream by the Spirit of God. He
warned Pharaoh of the seven years of drought that would
come on the earth, after the seven years of plenty. Pharaoh
made him the "number-two" man in Egypt in one day.
When the seven years of drought began, Egypt had suffi-
cient food in storage because of the wisdom of God
expressed through Joseph. When Jacob saw there was grain
in Egypt, he sent his sons—the ones who threw Joseph into
the pit and sold him into slavery—there to obtain food. If
Joseph had been an angry man, bitter and unforgiving, he
would have killed his brothers in revenge for what they
had done to him. But instead, he was a **place of refuge** for
his family. Look at what he said to his brothers:

And Joseph said unto his brethren, Come
near to me, I pray you. And they came near.
And he said, I [am] Joseph your brother,
**whom ye sold into Egypt. Now therefore
be not grieved, nor angry with yourselves,
that ye sold me hither: for God did send me
before you to preserve life.** For these two
years [hath] the famine [been] in the land:

> and yet [there are] five years, in the which
> [there shall] neither [be] earing nor harvest.
> And God sent me before you to preserve
> you a posterity in the earth, and to save your
> lives by a great deliverance. **So now [it was]
> not you [that] sent me hither, but God:** and
> he hath made me a father to Pharaoh, and
> lord of all his house, and a ruler throughout
> all the land of Egypt. [Emp. added]
>
> Genesis 45:4-8

Instead of Joseph getting revenge on the brothers who sold him to slavery, he blessed them by providing food and shelter. He overcame evil with good! His brothers' lives were changed, and the envy and wickedness had been devoured by the character of God that had been worked in Joseph's life.

In King David's case, the ending was different. Saul died in judgment. He never repented, but rather grew worse in his deception. But look at the way David responded to the death of Saul:

> Then David took hold on his clothes, and
> rent them; and likewise all the men that
> [were] with him: And they **mourned,** and
> **wept,** and **fasted** until even, **for Saul,** and
> for Jonathan his son, and for the people of
> the LORD, and for the house of Israel;
> **because they were fallen by the sword.**
> [Emp. added]   II Samuel 1:11-12

David then taught the men of Judah "The Song of the Bow." He was not rejoicing over the death of the man who once served God; in fact, he mourned over the man who once spent years chasing him to kill him. How could David do this? Because he was a broken man who had been tried in the furnace of affliction and come forth purified.

You may be going through the fire now. It appears that those among you whom you would expect to love you instead intend to do you harm. How will you respond? Will you defend or avenge yourself? Or will you allow God to avenge you? Will you keep yourself in the love of God? Will you be like David, who said:

> False witnesses did rise up; they laid to my charge [things] that I knew not. They rewarded me evil for good [to] the spoiling of my soul. **But as for me,** when they were sick, my clothing [was] sackcloth: I humbled my soul with fasting; and my prayer returned into mine own bosom. **I behaved myself as though [he had been] my friend [or] brother:** I bowed down heavily, as one that mourneth [for his] mother. [Emp. added]   Psalm 35:11-14

Remember, "Bless them which persecute you: bless, and curse not. . . . Recompense to no man evil for evil. . . . avenge not yourselves, but [rather] give place unto wrath: for it is written, **Vengeance [is] mine**; I will repay, saith the Lord. Therefore if thine enemy hunger, feed him; if he thirst, give him drink: for in so doing thou shalt heap coals of fire on his head. **Be not overcome of evil, but overcome evil with good**" (Romans 12:14, 17, 19-21). Vengeance is God's—not ours! We must, as Joseph, overcome evil with good.

DO NOT AVENGE YOURSELVES WITH BITTERNESS, UNFORGIVENESS, GOSSIP, SLANDER, OR STRIFE. BUT RATHER PUT ON THE LOVE OF GOD, FOR LOVE COVERS THE MULTITUDE OF SINS!

SECTION

4

TIME OF PREPARATION

CHAPTER 12

PREPARE THE WAY OF THE LORD

*. . . where you are presently is a
vital part of where you are going.*

The voice of him that crieth in the wilderness, **Prepare ye the way of the LORD,**
make straight in the desert a highway for
our God. **Every valley** shall be **exalted,** and
every mountain and hill shall be made **low:**
and the **crooked** shall be made straight, and
the **rough** places **plain:** And **the glory of the
LORD shall be revealed,** and all flesh shall
see [it] together: for the mouth of the LORD
hath spoken [it]. The voice said, Cry. And he
said, What shall I cry? All flesh [is] grass,
and all the goodliness thereof [is] as the
flower of the field: The grass withereth, the
flower fadeth: because the spirit of the
LORD bloweth upon it: surely the people
[is] grass. The grass withereth, the flower
fadeth: but the word of our God shall stand
for ever. [Emp. added]   Isaiah 40:3-8

The desert, or wilderness, is the place where **the way of the Lord is prepared,** the place where every mountain is made low and every valley exalted. In scripture, mountains represent the strength of man. The Bible says, "That no flesh should glory in His presence" (I Corinthians 1:29). Man cannot bring forth the promises of God. No matter how good his intentions, without God's involvement man can do nothing of eternal value—even in Jesus' name. Jesus said, "The Son can do **nothing of himself, but what he seeth the Father do**" [Emp. added] (John 5:19). What a statement! Jesus said *He* could do *NOTHING* of Himself.

Jesus loved Lazarus and his two sisters, Martha and Mary, who lived in Bethany. Lazarus became very ill. John 11:3-6 says, "Therefore his sisters sent unto him, saying, 'Lord, behold, he whom thou lovest is sick.' When Jesus heard [that], he said, 'This sickness is not unto death, but **for the glory of God,** that the Son of God might be glorified thereby.' Now Jesus loved Martha, and her sister, and Lazarus. **When he had heard therefore that he was sick, he abode two days still in the same place where he was**" [Emp. added]. Jesus loved Lazarus and considered him a friend. However, we see that Jesus did nothing for two days. Why didn't He go immediately to Bethany? The reason: God did not lead Him to go immediately. Jesus waited until the Spirit of God moved; then He moved. The Lord showed me that if that had been one of my friends whom I loved, I would have driven immediately to his house and laid hands on him, without even thinking of looking to the Spirit of God for His direction. We have had the mentality in the Church that, "Wherever I go, God will go—and do what I tell Him to do." This is backward thinking. *God* decides where to go; if we follow, He will tell *us* what to do. We have thought that even without the Spirit's leading, if we laid hands on the sick, God was obligated to heal everyone of them at that moment. If this is true, then we should go to all the hospitals and empty them. In many references in the Bible it says, "He healed them all." But this was not a universal occurrence. For instance, why didn't Jesus heal all the sick, blind, lame, and paralyzed people at the pool of Bethesda when He healed the man with the infirmity for thirty-eight years (John 5)? Why did He only heal one man at that time?

There was a man, lame from his mother's womb, who was laid daily at the gate of the temple. Surely Jesus passed him each time He entered the temple. Why didn't Jesus heal him? Because His Father hadn't instructed Him to do so. Later, on the way to the temple, Peter and John (by the leading of the Spirit) healed this man, causing revival to break out (Acts 3).

When Jesus ministered, there was no set formula; some He spit on, some He laid hands on, others He simply spoke to. He made mud balls for another and put them in his eye sockets; still others He sent to the priests, and the list goes on. Why such variety? Because He only did what He saw His Father do! God knew the perfect timing and manner in which each individual could receive healing.

This is what God wants for His servants . . . to bring them to the place **where they will do only what they see Him do, not what they think or want to be done.** Jesus said in John 20:21, ". . . as my Father hath sent me, even so send I you." As Jesus did nothing except what He was seeing the Father do, even so we must do only what we see the Lord do. We must behave as Jesus, led only by the Holy Spirit, walking as only He can lead us. This requires our flesh to be under subjection to the Spirit of God. The training ground for this Spirit-led life is the wilderness. As earlier noted, the wilderness is where the **way of the Lord** is prepared.

In the body of Christ in these last days, there are many with a genuine call to full-time ministry, but before God releases them, He first will bring them by way of the wilderness for a season of preparation. In the wilderness, the flesh is crucified and the **way of the Lord** is prepared. Look at the life of Moses:

> Now when he [Moses] was forty years
> old, **it came into his heart** to visit his
> brethren, the children of Israel, and seeing
> one of [them] suffer wrong, he defended and
> avenged him who was oppressed, and
> struck down the Egyptian. **For he supposed**
> **that his brethren would have understood**
> **that God would deliver them by his hand,**
> but they did not understand. [Emp. added]
>   Acts 7:23-25 (NKJV)

At forty, Moses knew he was called to deliver Israel
from Egyptian bondage. He had been raised as a prince,
trained in the wisdom and knowledge of Egypt. At that
time, Egypt was the greatest nation on earth. No other
nation was as advanced. If anyone was qualified to lead not
only Israel, but also Egypt, it was Moses.

Moses, endeavoring to show his leadership ability
and his faithfulness to Israel, killed an Egyptian who was
oppressing one of the men of Israel. His attempt to validate himself in this way failed, and suddenly we see
God's "mighty deliverer" fleeing to Midian for his own
life. There he was kept busy tending another man's sheep
on the back side of the desert. Not for just a few years,
but for forty years! Why would a man called by God
"waste" forty years in the desert? God was causing the
mountain of flesh to be brought low, the crooked places
made straight, and the rough places made smooth. *The*
Lord's way was being prepared.

After Moses has endured forty humbling years of refining, God appears:

> Come now therefore, and **I will send**
> **thee** unto Pharaoh, that thou mayest bring
> forth my people the children of Israel out of
> Egypt. And Moses said unto God, '**Who am**
> **I, that I should go unto Pharaoh, and that I**

**should bring forth the children of Israel
out of Egypt?'** [Emp. added] Exodus 3:10-11

Is this the same Moses, who forty years previously, without God's direction, had tried to deliver Israel? Now there he stood in the presence of God, commissioned to go, and he was afraid. Moses had been humbled to the point that he knew if God was not involved, he again would fail miserably. Having been rejected once as deliverer, he now looked for God to validate him. His first attempt had been in the strength of his own ability. It was Moses' way, even though it was in response to a genuine call. The greatness of Egypt's wisdom could not prepare Moses. (Egypt is symbolic of the world system, and the world's wisdom can never prepare us for the mission to which God has called us.) It was the barren lonely backside of the desert which prepared Moses for the task that lay ahead. Now he was ready to deliver Israel God's way.

Notice the word of the Lord, **"I will send thee."** Moses had "sent" himself forty years earlier, but now God was sending Moses!

In 1979, I was born again while in my college fraternity. Four months later, I was filled with the Holy Spirit. God began to deal with me concerning the ministry. I did not want anything to do with the ministry. All the ministers I had met appeared to be men who were slow in life. I viewed them as ignorant, with strange kids and old, dirty houses. (I had never met any good ones). My idea of ministry was warped at best. I thought to be a minister I'd have to be like them or end up in Africa living in a shack with no shoes on.

My plans at the time were to complete my studies of Mechanical Engineering at Purdue University, followed with an MBA from Harvard. I avoided God's dealings concerning the ministry. But four months later as I was sitting in church on Sunday morning, the Spirit of God came on me and very sternly said, "I have called you to preach! What are you going to do about it?" I said, "Lord, even if I end up in Africa in a shack with no shoes I will preach. I will obey You!" (God has His way of getting our attention.) As soon as I said "Yes" to the call, the Lord began to prepare me. The fire began to burn; I told my fraternity brothers about Jesus and many got saved. About a year and a half later, I started a Bible study in the fraternity. People came from all over the campus. Every week new people came and were saved, filled with the Spirit, and healed. Now the desire to preach was strong—I wanted to quit Purdue and go to Bible school. My reasoning? Why study thermal dynamics when I am called to preach, and people out there are dying and going to hell? Jesus could return soon and I must go to the harvest fields as soon as possible. One night as I was doing the homework I despised, I looked from my engineering book to the Bible on the shelf, and, throwing my engineering book against the wall, I determined I would quit school and go to Bible college. I called a Purdue researcher who was discipling me and said, "Don, I'm leaving and going to Bible school!" He wisely said, "Why don't we go out and pray about it tonight." We did and God spoke to me and said, "In my appointed time." The Lord later went on to say, "Who has ordained this ministry, you or me?" I said, "You have, Lord." He said, "Don't you think I am more concerned about this ministry coming forth than even you?"

So I finished engineering and moved to Dallas, Texas. There I was a member of a church of seven thousand people. I began to usher in the church and help in any areas of need. I began to attend their night Bible school. Two years later I was hired as an assistant. I told them I only could commit to one year because I was called to preach. My job was to wash and fill their cars with gas, shine the pastor's shoes, run errands, pick up their children from school, give swimming lessons to two preschoolers, and many other tasks. I was not there one year, but for four and a half.

Eight years now had gone by since I had said "Yes" to the call of God. In college, watching all those students saved, healed, and delivered, I thought the full-time ministry was just days away. I had no idea about the process through which God would bring me. But there I was in the wilderness for several years.

During the period of time I served, I tried unsuccessfully three times to get into full-time preaching ministry. As I flew back to Dallas from Asia (after the third try to see if that was where God wanted me), I was reading the gospel of John, when I came to the sixth verse in chapter one and saw this, "There was a man **sent from God**, whose name was John" [Emp. added]. The words "sent from God" jumped off the page and God said to me, "Do you want to be sent by John Bevere or do you want to be sent by God?" I said, "I want to be sent by God." And the Lord said, "Good, because if you are sent by John, you'll go in John's authority, but if you are sent by God, you will go in my authority!" After this, I began to settle down and enjoy where God had placed me. While I was out praying one morning I said, "Lord, if You return and I'm still driving this van and running errands for my pastor and his wife, I know I can look at You and say, 'I have obeyed You.'" Six months later I was a youth pastor in a large church in Florida.

Had God put me on a shelf for those eight years until some position opened up? NO! A thousand times no! I had been brought to that wilderness in order to develop godly character . . . that *His way* might be prepared. My character needed to be developed in order to function in the call of that position of ministry. The process was complete for that level of ministry. However, with every spiritual promotion, first must come the preparation for that level.

God said to Moses after forty years of wilderness training:

> Come now therefore, and **I will send thee** unto Pharaoh, that thou mayest bring forth my people the children of Israel out of Egypt. And Moses said unto God, Who am I, that I should go unto Pharaoh, and that I should bring forth

the children of Israel out of Egypt? And he
said, **Certainly I will be with thee;** . . . [Emp.
added]   Exodus 3:10-12

Look at what God said about preachers that sent themselves: "**I have not sent** these prophets, **yet they ran: I have
not spoken to them, yet they prophesied** . . . yet I sent
them not, nor commanded them: therefore they shall not
profit this people at all, saith the LORD" [Emp. added]
(Jeremiah 23:21,32).

Moses was not able to help or *profit* the children of Israel
when he attempted to deliver them at the age of forty. God
had not yet sent him. Even with all of Egypt's wisdom,
without God's wisdom and timing he could not fulfill
God's call. It was not God's appointed time! His vain effort
only resulted in the death of one Egyptian oppressor. But at
the appointed time, when Moses was sent by God, an entire
army lay beneath the Red Sea. That is the difference
between our strength and God's strength.

John the Baptist trained thirty years for a six-month
ministry, yet Jesus said he was the greatest prophet born of
woman. God can do more in six months through a man or
woman *sent by Him* than can someone else working hard *in
their own strength* for eighty years.

At forty, Moses knew he had a commission from God.
Even though his intentions were noble, his intial attempt
did more harm than good. After forty years of backside
desert training, a new Moses emerges who will do nothing
except what God has told him. Sound familiar? It is what
Jesus said: "Verily, verily, I say unto you, The **Son can do
nothing of himself, but what he seeth the Father do:** . . ."
[Emp. added] (John 5:19).

Look again at Isaiah 40:3-8:

The voice of him that crieth in the wilderness, **Prepare ye the way of the LORD,**
make straight in the desert a highway for

our God. Every **valley** shall be exalted, and
every **mountain and hill** shall be made low:
and the **crooked** shall be made straight, and
the **rough** places plain: And the glory of the
LORD shall be revealed, and all flesh shall
see it together: for the mouth of the LORD
hath spoken it. The voice said, Cry. And he
said, What shall I cry? **All flesh [is] grass,
and all the goodliness thereof is as the
flower of the field: The grass withereth, the
flower fadeth**: because the spirit of the
LORD bloweth upon it: surely the people is
grass. The grass withereth, the flower
fadeth: **but the word of our God shall stand
for ever.** [Emp. added]   Isaiah 40:3-8

God is saying that the wilderness is where **the way of
the Lord** is prepared. The way of the Lord is not the
strength of man. He says that the pride of flesh shall be
made low, the humble (those who wait on the Lord) exalted, the crooked places made straight, and rough places
made smooth. As a college student, I had tapped into flowing in the anointing, but there were mountains in my life to
be made low and rough and crooked places to be made
smooth and straight. God began His processing in the
wilderness. In our wilderness period, it is important to
allow God to have His way in our lives. While I was in the
position of serving my pastor in Dallas, the Lord spoke to
me one day and said, "John, don't miss what I want to do in
you today by only looking for the preaching ministry of
tomorrow." I so badly wanted to preach, that I viewed this
phase of my life as a waste of time. Don't fall into this trap.
Realize that God is not *wasting time!* He is the one who
redeems time! Realize that where you are presently is a vital
part of where you are going. It is your training arena. Let
Him worry about how it will all work out and come together . . . you just flow! He is God, the Author and Finisher. All

we are to do is trust Him and obey what He is showing us
TODAY! Every time I thought I had figured out how He
was going to put me in the preaching ministry, He would
say, "John, you have just figured out another way it will not
happen!" This was true; the way He brought it forth was
totally unexpected. I'm sure Joseph never expected to find
his dream being fulfilled the way it actually happened.

God brings us to the place in which we are content (not
complacent) where we are. It will seem almost as if the
dream has died. But it is when *your* plans for fulfillment of
the dream die in your mind, will, and emotions that He prepares to resurrect them *His* way. I was puzzled and frustrated by what He had done with me. I asked, "Why did You
get me all excited about the ministry, when eight years later
I have to put the dream as an Isaac on the altar?" The Lord
answered, "Son, to reveal whether you are serving the
dream or me."

This is what God did with Abraham. He got him all excited, told him he would be the father of nations . . . and twenty-
five years later the promise began to come to pass. Then thirteen years later, after Abraham had loved and enjoyed Isaac,
his promised son, God tested him, telling him to put the
dream on the altar. God allowed that dream to die in
Abraham's mind, will, and emotions. Then He would see if
Abraham loved the dream more than the dream-Giver.

When God gives His authority and power to a man, the
mightier the authority and power given, the greater the judgment for not obeying the Spirit of the Lord. God did not judge
Moses at forty when he did things his own way, because
God's authority and power were not yet on him. However,
later this was not the case. While in the wilderness of Zin, the
people contended with Moses and complained about the
place to which he had brought them. They were thirsty and
wanted water. So God told Moses what to do:

> And the LORD spake unto Moses, say-
> ing, Take the rod, and gather thou the assem-

bly together, thou, and Aaron thy brother,
and **speak** ye unto the rock before their eyes;
and it shall give forth his water, . . . [Emp.
added]   Numbers 20:7-8

God told Moses to SPEAK to the rock and it would give
the water. But read what Moses did:

And Moses lifted up his hand, and with
his rod he **smote the rock twice:** and the
water came out abundantly, and the congregation drank, and their beasts [also]. And
the LORD spake unto Moses and Aaron,
**Because ye believed me not, to sanctify me
in the eyes of the children of Israel, therefore ye shall not bring this congregation
into the land which I have given them.**
[Emp. added]   Numbers 20:11-12

Notice God gave the water even though Moses dis-
obeyed God's instructions for calling it forth. The water
was for the people; it was in response to their need. So God
did not hold back the water from the people in order to
punish Moses; what He did do was prevent Moses from
leading the people into the promised land, since he had not
honored God before them. (Moses hit the rock rather than
speaking to it, thus making himself the focus of the people)
This is a perfect example of how the supernatural anointing
of God is for the needs of the people, not to exalt the minister or to raise money. With all the misuse of the gifts,
anointing, and scriptures recently, many have decided that
the gifts, the promises, and the power are invalid. This is
not true, but God is looking for a new breed of leadership
which will sanctify Him before the people. It is possible for
ministers to have a valid gifting or anointing that will meet
the needs of the people, yet be in disobedience on their pre-
sentation of that gifting.

Possibly, Moses was frustrated with the people and a little frustrated with God because the water didn't come out
immediately. Moses struck the rock, as he had done previously in the wilderness of Sin (Exodus 17:1-7). Or perhaps
Moses had become comfortable with his ability to lead;
maybe he now felt God would honor whatever he deemed
best. Once again he had done something his own way, but
this time the consequences were considerably greater.
Moses had walked in the power and might of God; all his
strength was from his dependency on God. Now for Moses
to act independently of God before the people brought
judgment and punishment. God said that because of his
actions, he and Aaron would not bring the children of Israel
into the promised land.

That is why James 3:1 says, "My brethren, let not many
of you become teachers, knowing that we shall receive a
stricter judgment." **The greater the glory, the greater the
judgment.**

King Saul spared the king of Amalek and a few sheep.
He was more concerned with what the people wanted than
what God had commanded. His poor judgment cost him
the kingdom. King David measured his own strength by
numbering the children of Israel, bringing judgment on the
entire nation.

The wilderness prepares us to walk in the power and
glory of the Lord, without the sin and resulting judgment of
disobedience. Pride is made low and humility is exalted.
The truly humble man walks as Jesus walked, crying, "I
will not do anything unless I see the Spirit of the Lord do it.
I am nothing in my own strength and ability."

The reason God has withheld the manifestation of his
glory and power from the Church is to protect us from
greater judgment. He is stripping the flesh from the spirit in
the wilderness, to cause us to cry out for Him. Then when
His glory manifests itself, we will sanctify His name by
doing things only HIS WAY!

Preacher, don't do something just because someone else

did and it was successful. Don't copy another's ministry. Don't do something just because it is traditional. Don't do something because it is commonly accepted today in the ministry. Hear the voice of the Spirit. Let Him show you how He wants the ministry conducted. See and hear what the Lord is doing and saying.

> I will stand upon my watch, and set me upon the tower, and **will watch to see what he will say unto me**, and what I shall answer when I am reproved. And the LORD answered me, and said, '**Write the vision, and make it plain upon tables, that he may run that readeth it.** For the vision is yet for an **appointed time**, but at the end it shall speak, and not lie: though it tarry, wait for it; because it will surely come, it will not tarry. **Behold, his soul which is lifted up is not upright in him: but the just shall live by his faith.** [Emp. added]   Habakkuk 2:1-4

The prophet said, "I will watch to see what God will say unto me." One of the ways the Spirit of God speaks is through vision. Jesus said He only did what He SAW the Father doing. Habakkuk said he would write what he saw and run with what he saw at the appointed time. He went on to say that the soul which is proud (lifted up) is not upright (that is the man who does not **wait** on the word of the Lord, but runs without the vision of what God is saying). But the just shall live by **his** faith, not by **another's** faith! Faith comes by hearing what God is saying. That is why God brought the children of Israel into the wilderness. ". . . that He might make you know that man shall not live by bread alone; but man lives by every word that **proceeds** from the mouth of the Lord" [Emp. added] (Deuteronomy 8:3). Notice He said **proceeds** and not **proceeded**. It is the word that He is **saying**, not **said**.

We are admonished in Hebrews 12:25 (NKJV): "See that you do not refuse Him who **speaks** [present tense]. For if they did not escape who refused Him who spoke on earth, much more shall we not escape if we turn away from Him who **speaks** from heaven, . . ." [Emp. added]. But never forget, what He speaks will always line up with the written scriptures. However, searching the scriptures to back up what *you* think should be done still is not God's way. Jesus could have said to himself, "I am anointed to heal the sick, so I'll go at once to lay hands on Lazarus as I have done before." Instead, He waited for the Spirit of God to move; then He moved. Let us follow His example, being led by the Spirit to do things *God's* way and not *our* way.

The wilderness is where God brings us to teach us that any attempt to do something for Him, apart from His leading and ability, is an exercise in futility. When we truly learn that the flesh can do nothing worthy of eternal value, then we are ready for the ministry to which He has called us. The wilderness is preparation for future ministry.

CHAPTER 13

PREPARATION FOR CHANGE

The wilderness is where God brings forth a fresh move of His Spirit.

Remember ye not the former things, neither consider the things of old. Behold, I will do a **new thing;** now it shall **spring forth;** shall ye not know it? I will even make **a way in the wilderness,** and rivers in the desert. [Emp. added]   Isaiah 43:18

The wilderness is where God brings forth a fresh move of His Spirit. Of course, it is not new to God, but it is to us. We have yet to arrive where we know Him as He knows us. This type of relationship is described in II Corinthians 3:18: "But we all, with open face beholding as in a glass [mirror] the glory of the Lord, are **changed** into the same image **from glory to glory,** even as by the Spirit of the Lord" [Emp. added]. In order to know Him, we must **change.** Changes that brings us closer to Him often are not easy, but they are always good. Often we resist change because it affects our comfort level. Humans are creatures of habit.

Once these patterns are established it becomes uncomfortable to move outside this life-style. This happens especially in the area of religion. Religious strongholds and traditions are formed early and run deep. Not all traditions are wrong, but when a person responds merely from tradition and not from his heart, then he is going through lifeless motions. A person who has a religious spirit is one who has an outward form of godliness, holding fast to what God DID, while resisting what God is DOING presently.

We see this type of behavior in the Pharisees and other religious leaders of Jesus' day. They boasted that they were Abraham's children and sons of the covenant. They claimed to be disciples of Moses. Holding fast to what God DID, they resisted the Son of God standing in their midst. They were zealous for their traditions and manner of worship; however, when Jesus came, He challenged every area of comfort and stability, He made them realize God wasn't going to fit into their box . . . they would have to fit in His. They resisted this change and clung to their traditions. A religious spirit will breed an elitist attitude (God will operate only through us and within our parameters), which will result in prejudice and, eventually, hatred and betrayal if it is not checked. This is exactly what happened in Jesus' time and has happened throughout Church history.

In order to change and make the transition from one level of glory to the next, we must be willing to leave our comfort zone and pursue the way that the Spirit of the Lord leads us. This path will lead through a wilderness where God causes new life to spring forth.

This is apparent in the life of John the Baptist. His father was a priest—a high priest at one time. John's inheritance was to become a priest, as his father. He was to go to school in Jerusalem and study under Gamaliel to become a Pharisee. But one day the Spirit of the Lord began to call John to the wilderness. The more John would pray, the stronger the inward urge to go to the wilderness. A conflict began to arise within him as he thought to himself, my friends that I've grown up with are going to 'Bible School.' They will get diplomas and be recognized as leaders. They will be ordained and have the ability to preach in every synagogue in the country. What will they think of me? How will I ever fulfill this call on my life if I don't go to 'Bible School'? I know there is a call on my life. My dad told me an angel announced my birth and told him I would be a minister, but if I go out to this wilderness, nobody will ever know who I am. I'll never get invited to preach." However, the burning call to the wilderness he felt within him overrode the questions bombarding his mind, and he decided to follow the Spirit to the wilderness. We read in Luke 1:80, "And the child grew, and waxed strong in spirit, and was in the **deserts** till the day of his shewing unto Israel" [Emp. added].

Luke 3:2-3 says, ". . . the word of God came unto John the son of Zacharias **in the wilderness**. And he came into all the country about Jordan, preaching the baptism of repentance for the remission of sins; . . ." [Emp. added]. It was in the wilderness that God prepared John, not in the accepted "Bible School" of his day! All the land of Judea and those from Jerusalem went out to him to hear the word of the Lord. A new move of the Spirit was beginning to blow, but across the *desert*, not in the *religious places*. Those who were fed up with the religious hypocracy and traditions went out to John, with hearts willing to change in preparation for the appearing of God's Son.

Soon after this, Jesus came to be baptized by John in the Jordan river. Even though John protested this, Jesus insisted he do it. It was necessary for Jesus' ministry to come forth from what the Spirit of God was doing presently on the earth. Jesus was then filled with the Spirit and was immediately led into the wilderness. The Bible is very clear that when Jesus was led into the wilderness, He was *filled* **with the Spirit,** but after the forty days of testing and temptation, He returned from the wilderness **in the *power* of the Spirit.** Now He was equipped for the ministry for which

He came. After only a few months of John the Baptist's ministry, another new thing was sprung forth from the wilderness—the ministry of Jesus Christ.

Now at the beginning of Jesus' ministry, the disciples of John the Baptist came to Jesus and said to Him, "Why do the disciples of John fast often, and make prayers, and likewise the disciples of the Pharisees; but thine eat and drink?" (Luke 5:33). These men were a little annoyed because they fasted from food often, and Jesus' disciples did not fast at all. They were doing all the sacrificing, yet Jesus' disciples were getting all the attention. So we can see that one of the ways the Spirit of God was moving in John's day was through much fasting. However, these men had not made the transition or change from the ministry of John to what the Spirit of God *now* was doing. They believed their *method* of ministry and worship was what had brought the fruit. They had paid a great price to follow John the Baptist. They had sacrificed much, and now their leader was in prison . . . and here comes this new Man Who has disciples with Him who don't play by their rules. These men were offended and in danger of developing a religious spirit. Remember, religious spirits always will hold on to what God DID, while they resist what He is DOING. Why? It is possible that at one point they became more concerned about with whom they were affiliated and how their affiliates behaved than with what God was saying and doing *now*. Their focus was no longer the heart of God. The *method*, which at one time may have led to His heart, now became their focus. Pride and offense began to dominate. They had invested time, and possibly money, into the ministry, and now all that they had done, or stood for, or obtained was threatened. So they began to maintain the methods and resist the change, even though John, the leader of these men, declared, "He must increase, but I must decrease" (John 3:30).

Look at how Jesus answers them: "And he said unto them, Can ye make the children of the bridechamber fast, while the bridegroom is with them?" (Luke 5:34). He expos-es their religious ways by saying, "Why would they need to go on a fast when the Son of God is standing in their midst? All they need to do if they need something from God is come to me!" (paraphrased). Religious thinking caused them to believe they had to earn God's favor through fasting, etc. They began to see fasting as a means of access to God, which they felt raised them above others who did not fast (or use their methods, whatever they may have been); thus, pride began to settle in. So the method became more important than its original fruit. Though there is benefit to fasting, fast-ing from food is not a way to manipulate God, but to bring *you* into a position to hear easily what God is saying or doing. So why should the disciples have had to fast to hear God's voice, when He was right there with them?

Look again at Luke 5:34-35: "And he said unto them, Can ye make the children of the bridechamber fast, while the bridegroom is with them? But the days will come, when **the bridegroom shall be taken away** from them, and **then shall they fast in those days**" [Emp. added]. He does not say that they **might** fast in those days. He says they **will** fast in those days. These men were talking about only fasting from food, but Jesus talks to them about a different fast. Notice this fast will be in the days that the **Bridegroom is taken away**. He is talking about a fast **of His presence**, not only a fast from food. The reason we know this is because He explains it in the parable He is about to give in the next few verses. A fast of His presence is the wilderness. In light of this, remember, one of the definitions of the wilderness is the absence of the tangible presence of God.

Now look at the parable He gives to explain what He is saying:

> . . . No man putteth a piece of a new gar-ment upon an old; if otherwise, then both the new maketh a rent, and the piece that was [taken] out of the new agreeth not with the

old. And no man putteth new wine into old
bottles; else the new wine will burst the bottles, and be spilled, and the bottles shall perish. But new wine must be put into new bottles; and both are preserved.   Luke 5:36-38

In the Bible, new wine is an example of God's presence.
Paul said in Ephesians 5:18, "And do not be drunk with wine
in which is dissipation; but be filled with the Spirit, . . ." We
are to be filled with the new wine!

Remember when you first were filled with the Spirit
how wonderful it was? God's presence was sweet and
strong. Every time you would pray, His presence immediately would manifest itself. You would sense His presence
all day long. At times in church you would just sit and cry
because of His presence. Then one day much later, you
notice that you don't sense it quite so easily. You still are
praying like you used to, but you are thinking, "Where is
God?" You have arrived at a wilderness. There is a reason
for that wilderness or fast of God's presence. God is preparing the new wine skin. You can't put new wine, which is a
fresh move of God's spirit, into old wine skins.

To better understand this, we must look at the wine
skins they used in Jesus' day. These wine bottles or vessels
were made of sheepskin. When the wine first was put in,
the skins were flexible and pliable. They stretched easily
and would yield without resistance. However, as the years
went by the atmosphere would absorb all the moisture out
of the wine skin, leaving it brittle and hard. Now if the wine
was poured out and new wine poured in, the skin could
handle neither the weight of the new wine nor the fermen-
tation process, because it was now rigid and brittle and
could break easily. What they did was soak the skin in
water for several days and then rub olive oil on it. That
made it flexible and pliable again. This is symbolic of what
happens to us, for we are the vessels of the spiritual new
wine. Ephesians 5:26 says, "That He [Jesus] might sanctify

and cleanse it with the washing of water by the word." We must be soaked in the Word of God. Job said in his time of testing that he treasured the words of the Lord more than his necessary food (Job 23:12). The rubbing of olive oil comes from spending time seeking God in prayer. But in order to rejuvenate the old wine skin, you first have to **pour out the old wine!** That means no wine in the vessel—**no tangible presence of God!** That means a fast of the presence of God, or as we have been saying continually, that means a dry time!

Why does God remove His tangible presence? To get you frustrated? No! (Even though that will occur.) Is it because He wants to put you on the shelf until He has need of you? No!

The reason He withdraws His presence is to cause you to seek and search for Him. Seeking makes you flexible and pliable again. People who become rigid and inflexible are people who stop seeking God. They get set in their methods of ministry, in their methods of prayer, in their doctrine, etc. They are set in the formulas that they themselves have devised from previous experiences.

That was the condition of these men. They followed John because they could see the Lord was working mightily through him. However, instead of continuing to press on to the high call of knowing God, they became rigid in their beliefs and methods. In every move of God there is fresh teaching that comes forth. Teaching and doctrine is a means of bringing us to the heart of God. If we focus on the teaching or doctrine itself, then eventually it will bring us into religious bondage or legalism or error (or all of the above). You cannot know God through a formula. Many Christians have desired formulas. They get their seven steps to healing, their four steps to leading someone to salvation, their ten scriptures on prosperity, and so forth. Then when they finally have gotten the knowledge to be the "model Christian," they stop *seeking* and settle down into the tradition they have developed. Yet, somehow they feel empty, even if it is, TO THEM, the "full gospel."

Jeremiah 29:12-13 says, "Then shall ye call upon me, and ye shall go and pray unto me, and I will hearken unto you. And ye shall **seek** me, and find [me], when ye shall **search** for me with **all your heart**" [Emp. added]. Praying by itself is not enough to find Him. There are many who are bound by religious formulas who pray faithfully. God says that in your prayer there must be a diligent seeking of HIM. He clearly states here that there will be searching. There is no routine in searching. Searching takes effort. That is why God says in Hebrews 11:6, ". . . for he that cometh to God must believe that he is, and that he is a rewarder of them that **diligently seek him**" [Emp. added].

Now let's look again at what Jesus said in Luke 5:37-39: "And no man putteth new wine into old bottles; else the new wine will burst the bottles, and be spilled, and the bottles shall perish. But new wine must be put into new bottles; and both are preserved. **No man also having drunk old wine straightway desireth new: for he saith, The old is better**" [Emp. added]. No man who is used to the old wine will immediately desire the new wine. The key word here is "straightway" (**immediately**), because we are human beings with habit patterns and addictions. God must break those comfort zones by emptying the *old wine* and allowing us to go through a dry time of preparation with *no wine*, in order that we might become **thirsty** for the *new wine*. Jesus said in Matthew 5:6, "Blessed are they which do hunger and **thirst** after righteousness: for they shall be **filled**" [Emp. added]. When there is nothing at all to drink and you have become thirsty, you won't complain, "I don't want this wine, I want the old." Even so, if you are longing for the presence and power of God in your life, you will be open to the fresh move of God's Spirit in your life and ministry. You will be like David, who said in his wilderness time, "O God, thou art my God; early will I seek thee: my soul **thirsteth** for thee, my flesh longeth for thee in a **dry and thirsty land**, where no water is; To see thy power and thy glory, . . ." [Emp. added] (Psalm 63:1-2). David was thirsty for the power and presence of God. As a result, when he came into the ministry to which he was called, he was flexible to what the Lord desired—unlike king Saul who did things his own way and not God's.

The first preaching ministry I held was that of a youth pastor in Florida. We had a strong youth group. We were on two television stations every weekend in two states, with a potential viewing audience of more than four million. We had evangelistic radio spots on the second-most-popular secular station in the central Florida region. Everything was going great. Then one day in prayer the Spirit of God spoke that **change** was coming. He told me, "You will be removed from being youth pastor and I will send you to churches and cities from the east coast to the west coast of America; from the Canadian border to the Mexican border; to Alaska and Hawaii. . . ." He continued to show me what I would do in that next move of His Spirit in my life. I told my wife and the two of us pondered it in our hearts, not sharing it with anyone else. He said He would do it, and I knew that if it was truly Him, I wouldn't have to "help God."

It did not happen for eighteen months. During that waiting period, getting into God's presence became harder and harder, until it seemed impossible. I was spending more time in prayer than I had before, and still it seemed as if I were getting nowhere. Not only that, the vision I had for the youth group seemed to be fading (the old wine was being poured out). The more I prayed, the more the vision dwindled. Nothing had changed outwardly, but inwardly the desire was fading. I began to confess every sin I could recall that I may have committed, but there was no relief from the dryness I was experiencing. One day after trying to figure out exactly what sin it was that I had committed, the Lord spoke to me and said, "You are not in this desert because you have sinned; I'm preparing you for the change that is coming." I would spend hours in prayer before our youth services, and a couple of times I even begged God to get someone else to preach. I would go to the service, and God's presence would fall on me like a blanket while I ministered to the youth, and when I finished with the service, halfway home it would lift for another week! In the midst of all this, we went through internal and external trials as we had never experienced before.

After I had spent almost a year of going through this desert, the Lord put it in my heart to go on a food fast. After several days of this food fast, a prayer came out that my ears heard after my mouth said it. It was a cry from my heart that bypassed my mind. I said, "Lord, it doesn't matter if I am in the middle of the desert where there is no one or if I am preaching to millions, I'll do the same thing in both places. I will pursue your heart!" All of a sudden bells went off and I saw what He was doing! I said, "God, that is exactly what You have been doing in me. You have brought me to the place where I see You as my inheritance and my first love, not the ministry or anything else. So when the change comes I won't make an idol out of it. I won't leave You as my first love and love the ministry instead of You. My heart will stay right." Then I remembered what God said about David: "And when he had removed him [Saul], he raised up unto them David to be their king; to whom also he gave testimony, and said, **I have found David the son of Jesse, a man after mine own heart, which shall fulfil all my will**" [Emp. added] (Acts 13:22). Saul loved his ministry to the point of killing to keep it. David was not a man after a throne; he was a man after the heart of God. While in the wilderness, David had a chance to kill Saul twice to get the throne, and he was encouraged to do so by the man with him. If David's motives had been the same as Saul's, he would have killed for the throne that was promised to him by God through the prophet Samuel.

There are men and women today who will slander, gossip, or lie to get what God promised them. They are after the order of Saul. They are killing to keep their ministry or killing to get their ministry. God is looking for the "Davids" who have hearts after Him, not a position. The preparation of the old wine skin is the character of God. It is the character of God that can contain the pressure of the new wine of the Spirit (His anointing and presence). Character is developed by seeking the One we desire to emulate.

Several months after I received the word from the Lord about the change that was coming, my pastor walked into a meeting and said that the Lord had shown him that one of his pastors (there were ten on staff) would be traveling full time soon and would no longer serve on his staff. He said, "John Bevere, that man is you." A few months later, in a period of only three weeks, I received seven invitations to preach—one in California, one on the Mexican border in Texas, one on the East Coast, and another an hour from the Canadian border, as well as three others. I walked into my pastor's office to ask him what to do about them, and he said, "John, I told you the Lord had shown this to me; looks like your time is here." A short time later he laid hands on my wife and me, and we have been traveling full time since then!

The eighteen-month wilderness prepared us for the change God was bringing into our lives and ministry. In that time He developed within me the character I needed to handle the call of that phase of ministry. Now look at Isaiah 43:18-19 again:

> Remember ye not the former things [the old wine], neither consider the things of old. Behold, I will do a new thing; now it shall spring forth; shall ye not know it? I will even make a **way in the wilderness,** [and] rivers in the desert [Emp. added].

He birthed this ministry to America in a wilderness where there seemed no way, and where it looked as if things were getting worse and worse.

God will cause that *old* wine to dry up so that when the

new comes, and trials hit in the *new*, you won't desire to return to the *old*. He uses the wilderness to prepare us for change.

CHAPTER 14

RESISTANCE TO CHANGE

. . . to know Him as He knows us. Until we attain that goal, we should not be satisfied, . . .

Brethren, I count not myself to have apprehended: but [this] one thing [I do], forgetting those things which are behind, and reaching forth unto those things which are before, **I press toward** the mark for the prize of the high calling of God in Christ Jesus. [Emp. added]   Philippians 3:13-14

In order to pursue the mark or effect of the high call of God for our lives, the first thing we must settle in our hearts is that we haven't apprehended or attained it as yet. We are not perfected; we must continue to **change and grow**.

Paul wrote two-thirds of the New Testament and pioneered many of the gentile churches. His ministry spread to the whole world. Yet toward the end of his life he said, "I count not myself to have apprehended." He wasn't satisfied. He would not be satisfied until he reached the mark of the high call of God.

We see the same thing with Moses. He had a tremendous ministry, a congregation of three million, and was part of miraculous signs and wonders like no one else in the Old Testament. However, God said that Moses was the meekest (most teachable) man on all the earth. He did not count himself to have apprehended, but continued to press on to the high call of God. In order to grow and change, we must be teachable.

The second thing we must do to pursue the mark of the high call of God is forget those things (victories and defeats) which are behind! Again, we look at what God says in Isaiah 43:18: **"Remember ye not the former things, neither consider the things of old.** Behold, I will do a **new thing;** now it shall spring forth; shall ye not know it? I will even make a way in the **wilderness,** [and] rivers in the desert" [Emp. added].

Most agree that past failures, rejections, or sins, if dwelled upon, will hinder us from moving forward in Christ. However, the *triumphs* of our past will hold us back, as well. If we feel confident and sure of ourselves and begin to rely on past accomplishments to sustain and validate us, we will miss what God has for us in the present. This is exactly what God is saying in Isaiah 43. The former things were of Him. In order to reach forward to the goal of the high call, we must be ready to leave the ways in which God moved through us in the past. Paul said, "When I was a child, I spake as a child, I understood as a child, I thought as a child: but when I became a man, I put away childish things. For now we see through a glass, darkly; but then **face to face: now I know in part; but then shall I know even as also I am known"** [Emp. added] (I Corinthians 13:11-12).

A child is not wrong; he is just immature. When I was five years old, my whole world seemed to be Tonka trucks and Legos. A major accomplishment was saying the alphabet. I was seeing life through a dark glass. I couldn't see things clearly yet, because I was not mature enough to handle them.

When I was eighteen years old, tonka trucks were a thing of the past. Now, after years of maturing, I was seeing life through a glass that was not quite so dark, although it wasn't totally clear; my level and capacity for understanding had grown. When an eighteen-year-old acts like a five-year-old, it is abnormal. As we grow, we put away or forget former, childish ways and understandings. They are no longer useful or functional for our needs or enjoyment.

Likewise, while growing in the things of God, as when we progress through life's stages, we should put away former, immature things. Paul was saying, now we see God's ways and His glory dimly, but as we pursue the mark of the high call, we will see clearer until we see God face to face. In other words, we will know Him as He knows us!

What is the mark or goal of the high call? Paul answered it in the previous verse about the high call. Philippians 3:10 says, "That I may **know him**, and the **power of his resurrection**, and the **fellowship of his sufferings**, being made **conformable unto his death**; . . ." [Emp. added].

The mark of the high call of God is to be conformed into the image of His Son, Jesus Christ—to know Him as He knows us! Until we attain that goal, we should not be satisfied, so we must never cease to search for the heart of God.

In summation, we first must realize we have yet to attain the mark of the high call, and second, we must forget the former things.

The third thing we must do to pursue the mark of the high call of God in our lives is to "PRESS TOWARD THE MARK!" To PRESS implies there will be resistance or pressure. There is opposition to knowing Him. The greatest threat to the devil is a person conformed to the image of Jesus Christ. The forces of darkness will fight that harder than anything. When a person is conformed to the image of Christ, he is no longer alive to himself, but to the One who lives in him. He then enters into the high life of God's ways.

That is why Paul said that in order to know Him, we must know the fellowship of His sufferings. The suffering

of the flesh will bring forth death to self, which will bring
resurrection life!

I Peter 4:1-2 says, "Forasmuch then as Christ hath suffered for us in the flesh, arm yourselves likewise with the
same mind: for he that hath suffered in the flesh hath
ceased from sin; That he no longer should live the rest of his
time in the flesh to the lusts [desires] of men, but to the will
of God."

Those who have suffered in the flesh have ceased from
sin. They are the ones who have the character of Christ
working in them. This is the goal for which we should be
shooting. What are the sufferings of Christ? Many have
misunderstood. Religion has perverted the Word to the
point that many avoid it. Suffering is *not* dying of disease or
lacking the money to pay your bills. It is *not* going without
food for weeks so that God will be moved by your sacrifice.
Suffering is not sacrifice—it is obedience!

Peter answers the question of suffering in verse 2: "... so
that he no longer can spend the rest of his earthly life in har-
mony with **human desires** but in accordance with **God's
will**" (I Peter 4:2, Wms).

What is meant by the "sufferings of Christ" is going
God's way when our mind, emotions, or physical senses
are beckoning us to go the way of ease or pleasure. It is
also the conflict we meet when God tells *us* to go one way,
but our friends, family, coworkers, etc., desire to go
another way. We usually encounter this from people with
whom we are closest.

A classic example of this is when Peter disagreed with
Jesus about His death and burial:

> From that time forth began Jesus to shew
> unto his disciples, how that he must go unto
> Jerusalem, and suffer many things of the
> elders and chief priests and scribes, and be
> killed, and be raised again the third day.
> Then Peter took him, and began to rebuke

> Then Peter took him, and began to rebuke
> him, saying, Be it far from thee, Lord: this
> shall not be unto thee. But he turned, and
> said unto Peter, Get thee behind me, Satan:
> thou art an offence unto me, **for you are not
> mindful of the things of God, but the
> things of men.** [Emp. added]
>
> Matthew 16:21-23

Jesus declared to His disciples that He must go to
Jerusalem, suffer, be killed, and be raised on the third day.
Peter obviously didn't hear the "resurrection part" of what
Jesus said, or he wouldn't have been so troubled by the
statement Jesus made about His coming death.

Can't you hear Peter's thoughts? "Wait a minute, You
are the Messiah (it had just been revealed to him), and You
are supposed to set up the kingdom and restore Israel. I
have left my business, my wife, and family to follow You. I
have lost friends to follow You. I've invested time in this.
I've developed a reputation. The leaders of the synagogues
think You are crazy; the newspapers are constantly writing
articles about how controversial You are. You are considered by many established theologians to be a heretic. And
now You are talking about death. Where will that leave me?
All this time invested in following You, and I'll be left with
nothing but a bad reputation." Then he blurts out, "No,
Lord, you can't do this!" (paraphrased).

Jesus had to point out quickly that Peter's thoughts
were in accordance with the way worldly men would
think. The world is trained by Satan ("the god of this
world," II Corinthians 4:4) to look out for its own interests.
The kingdom of Heaven is just the opposite. So in order to
fulfill the will of God, we must go against the flow of men,
even if that means we have to go against a "brother in the
Lord" whose mind is not renewed to the will of God. Peter
was not a wicked man, but his thought process in this matter was conformed to the world, not to Christ.

Another example of this is the children of Israel spying out the land of Canaan. They had been in the wilderness for over a year when God told Moses to send men to spy out the "promised land" which He was giving them. Moses chose twelve leaders, one from each tribe. Two of them were Joshua and Caleb.

When they returned from spying out the land, they gave conflicting reports of what they saw and what they should do. Ten of the men said, "'. . . the people are strong that dwell in the land, and the cities are walled, and very great: and moreover we saw the children of Anak there. The Amalekites dwell in the land of the south: and the Hittites, and the Jebusites, and the Amorites, dwell in the mountains: and the Canaanites dwell by the sea, and by the coast of Jordan. . . . We are not able to go up against the people; for they are stronger than we.' And they brought up an evil report of the land . . ." (Numbers 13:28-32).

Caleb and Joshua brought back a different report: "And Caleb stilled the people before Moses, and said, Let us go up at once, and possess it; for we are well able to overcome it. . . . If the LORD delight in us, then he will bring us into this land, and give it us; a land which floweth with milk and honey. Only rebel not ye against the LORD, neither fear ye the people of the land; for they are bread for us: their defence is departed from them, and the LORD is with us: fear them not" (Numbers 13:30; 14:8-9).

All twelve went together and saw the same things. All saw the same land, cities, and people. Why did ten come back seeing it one way and two return seeing it another?

God said about Caleb and Joshua that they had a **different spirit** in that they **followed Him fully** (Numbers 14:24). In other words, they did not follow men's desires but God's will. This is the key to understanding why ten leaders saw the same things differently than Joshua and Caleb. The ten were more concerned about their comfort, security, and families than what God desired. They were living in accordance with the desires of men, not the will of God. Their lives were led by what would affect them, not the kingdom of God. This was true of the rest of the people as well, for they said, ". . . Would God that we had died in the land of Egypt! or would God we had died in this wilderness! And wherefore hath the LORD brought us unto this land, to fall by the sword, that our wives and our children should be a prey? were it not **better for us** to return into Egypt?" [Emp. added] (Numbers 14:2-3). They were more concerned about what would be better for themselves than what God desired!

As a result, they never saw the promised land. They never fulfilled the high call of God for their lives. Joshua and Caleb, however, had to PRESS on. The resistance they had to face came from their own "brothers." Look at what their own "brothers" wanted to do. "And all the congregation said to stone them [Caleb and Joshua] with stones" (Numbers 14:10).

The suffering Joshua and Caleb faced was the resistance of their own brothers, who had unrenewed minds and were still conformed to think and see things as the world does.

Paul said that he had to forget those things that were behind and PRESS on toward the goal of the high call of God. Look again at Isaiah 43:18-19: "Remember ye not the former things, neither consider the things of old. Behold, I will do a new thing; now it shall spring forth; shall ye not know it? I will even make a way in **the wilderness**, [and] rivers **in the desert**" [Emp. added]. The children of Israel were looking back to the days of Egypt, when their bellies were filled and there was some form of stability. Even though they had been slaves in Egypt, what they were facing now looked much more difficult than even their bondage.

That is a sad fact but still true today. There are many who would rather stay in their bondage than to PRESS on to the will of God. They fear the change ahead more than the familiar oppressive surroundings in which they presently find themselves. There are others who are satisfied with what God has done in the past and are unwilling to press on to new challenges. The will of God will bring life and liberty. It is the only way that brings true fulfillment. However, to press on to the high call will look impossible to the natural eye. God said He would do a new thing, but it would spring forth in the wilderness. In other words, as we follow the Spirit of God to what He desires, it will lead us into what appears to be an impossible wilderness. But what seems impossible to men is possible to God.

Oh, Christian, do not stop your pursuit of God when resistance comes. He will not lead you into the easy places. He will lead you into the tough places, because the greater the battle, the greater the victory. If you *love* your life, you will quit in the tough places. You will end your pursuit and settle down to a fruitless life-style. The only way to endure what lies ahead in the days to come is to *lose* your life. Revelation 12:11 says, "And they overcame him [the devil] by the blood of the Lamb, and by the word of their testimony; and **they loved not their lives unto the death**" [Emp. added]. Those who are concerned more about themselves than the will of God are those who love their own lives, and Jesus said, "For whosoever will save his life shall lose it: and whosoever will lose his life for my sake shall find it" (Matthew 16:25).

SECTION 5

VICTORY IN THE WILDERNESS

CHAPTER 15

PLACE OF REVELATION

... to change or make the transition, we must be willing to leave the comfortable, the secure, and the familiar ...

Hearken to me, ye that follow after righteousness, ye that **seek the LORD**: look unto the rock [whence] ye are hewn, and to the hole of the pit [whence] ye are digged. Look unto Abraham your father, and unto Sarah [that] bare you: **for I called him alone**, and blessed him, and increased him. For the LORD shall comfort Zion: he will comfort all her waste places; and **he will make her wilderness like Eden, and her desert like the garden of the LORD**; joy and gladness shall be found therein, thanksgiving, and the voice of melody. [Emp. added]

Isaiah 51:1-3

Abraham is called the father of all those who believe (Romans 4:11-16). Notice God said that He called him **alone**. We saw in the last chapter that in order to change or

141

make the transition, we must be willing to leave the comfortable, the secure and the familiar to be led by God's Spirit to a desert place. A transitional man must be willing to leave his natural, social, or religious inheritance to move on with the Spirit of God. Abraham had to leave his family, friends, and inheritance to fulfill God's calling. In order to know God, he had to come apart and follow God to the land that He would show him.

God blessed Abram (his name before God changed it) and increased him as a result of his obedience. However, when he left his comfortable surroundings and arrived at the land to which the Lord led him, there was a severe famine in progress. Now stop and think about it. God promises to bless Abram, make him a great nation, and make his name great. Abram forsakes all to follow the Lord, and when he comes to the land, the famine is so severe he has to go Egypt to dwell (Genesis 12:1-10). At this point, most of us would decide we had missed God and go back to the place we had just left. The difference is Abram did not let the circumstances around him affect his faith in God. He knew God was capable of multiplying in a famine, a lesson we all may soon learn.

God shows us great things that He intends to do through us in the future, and then He leads us straight into a wilderness to prepare us. Samuel prophesied that David would be declared the next king . . . yet shortly afterward, David was dwelling in caves and wandering in the wilderness in preparation for the throne.

Joseph dreamed of a great future. God was going to make a great leader out of him. His father, mother, and brothers would even bow down to him . . . then he spent the next seventeen years going from a pit to slavery to a dungeon.

At forty years of age, Moses was shown that he would deliver his brethren from the Egyptians (Acts 7:23-25). However, he spent the next forty years in the backside of the desert tending another man's sheep.

John the Baptist was called to be a great prophet. His

dad told him the vision of his calling. For several years afterward he was in the deserts of Judea.

Jesus was announced by the Father to be the Son of God before the multitudes at the Jordan river. The Spirit of God descended on him in bodily form. Immediately, He was led by the Spirit out to the desert.

As we have seen, the wilderness is the place where God tests us, humbles us, refines us, and works His character in us. **It is the preparation ground for future ministry.**

The most exciting thing about the wilderness is that it is the place where **God reveals himself in a fresh new way!** Notice again what Isaiah 51:3 says: "For the LORD shall comfort Zion: he will comfort all her waste places; and **he will make her wilderness like Eden, and her desert like the garden of the LORD;** joy and gladness shall be found therein, thanksgiving, and the voice of melody" [Emp. added]. The garden of Eden was the place where God revealed himself to Adam. It was the place where Adam and God had fellowship together.

Where was Moses when God revealed Himself to him in the burning bush?

> Now Moses kept the flock of Jethro his father in law, the priest of Midian: and he led the flock to the **backside of the desert,** and came to the mountain of God, even to Horeb. And the angel of the LORD appeared unto him in a flame of fire out of the midst of a bush: and he looked, and, behold, the bush burned with fire, and the bush was not consumed. And **Moses said, I will now turn aside, and see** this great sight, why the bush is not burnt. And **when the LORD saw that he turned aside to see,** God called unto him out of the midst of the bush, and said, Moses, Moses. And he said, Here am I. [Emp. added]   Exodus 3:1-4

Moses spent forty years in that wilderness. One day, **suddenly,** God revealed Himself to Moses in the burning bush, saying, "I Am Who I AM." Moses makes the statement, "I will now turn aside, and see this great sight."

In the wilderness you become hungry and thirsty for the Lord. Therefore, when God gets ready to reveal Himself, you can turn aside easily from the things of life toward Him.

It was in the wilderness, not in Bible School, that the Lord revealed Himself to John the Baptist. Luke 3:2-3 says, "... **the word of God came unto John the son of Zacharias in the wilderness.** And he came into all the country about Jordan, preaching the baptism of repentance for the remission of sins" [Emp. added].

It was in the wilderness of Arabia that God revealed the mysteries of the New Testament to Paul the apostle. Galatians 1:16-17 says, "**To reveal his Son in me,** that I might preach him among the heathen; immediately I conferred not with flesh and blood: Neither went I up to Jerusalem to them which were apostles before me; but **I went into Arabia,** and returned again unto Damascus" [Emp. added].

Where was John the apostle when he received "The Revelation of Jesus Christ"? Revelation 1:9 says, "I John, who also am your brother, and companion in tribulation, and in the kingdom and patience of Jesus Christ, was in the **isle that is called Patmos,** for the word of God, and for the testimony of Jesus Christ" [Emp. added]. It was on the deserted island of Patmos that he received "The Revelation of Jesus Christ."

God revealed Himself to Joseph in Pharaoh's dungeon. Joseph began to interpret dreams of the baker, the butler, and eventually Pharaoh himself.

God revealed Himself to David in the wilderness as his Shepherd, his Strength, his Shield, his Fortress, and in many other ways.

It is in the wilderness that the Lord reveals Himself to us in a fresh way. Isaiah 45:15 says, "Verily thou [art] a God that **hidest** thyself, O God of Israel, the Saviour" [Emp. added]. The Lord hides Himself to those who are not hungry for Him. But to those who seek and search for Him with all their hearts, He will reveal Himself to them. Remember, God said that He brought the children of Israel into the wilderness to humble them and cause them to hunger. However, instead of hungering for God as Joshua did, they hungered for the things that the Lord had removed from them. So when He came to reveal Himself to them, as He had done with Moses, they rejected Him.

In Deuteronomy, we find:

> And it came to pass, when ye heard the voice out of the midst of the darkness, (for the mountain did burn with fire), that ye came near unto me, [even] all the heads of your tribes, and your elders; And ye said, Behold, the LORD our God hath shewed us his glory and his greatness, and we have heard his voice out of the midst of the fire: we have seen this day that God doth talk with man, and he liveth. Now therefore why should we die? for this great fire will consume us: if we hear the voice of the LORD our God any more, then we shall die. For who [is there of] all flesh, that hath heard the voice of the living God speaking out of the midst of the fire, as we [have], and lived? Go thou near, and hear all that the LORD our God shall say: and speak thou unto us all that the LORD our God shall speak unto thee; and we will hear [it], and do [it].
> Deuteronomy 5:23-27

God desired to reveal Himself to them in the wilderness, as He had done with Moses, but they backed off and said to Moses, "You go and speak to the Lord and come to us and tell us all that He says and we will do it." They never did *know* Him, they only knew *about* Him. Therefore, they never could do as He commanded them. Because of not knowing Him, they never saw the land promised them. They died in the wilderness. When God brings us into a wilderness, it will be to test us, to see if we will hunger for Him as John, Moses, David, Joseph, Paul, and others did, or if we will hunger for comfort and pleasure.

In James it says:

> Ye ask, and receive not, because ye ask amiss, that ye may consume it upon your lusts [desires]. Ye adulterers and adulteresses, know ye not that the friendship of the world is enmity with God? whosoever therefore will be a friend of the world is the enemy of God. Do ye think that the scripture saith in vain, The spirit that dwelleth in us lusteth to envy? But he giveth more grace. Wherefore he saith, God resisteth the proud, but giveth grace unto the humble. Submit yourselves therefore to God. Resist the devil, and he will flee from you. **Draw nigh to God, and he will draw nigh to you. Cleanse [your] hands, [ye] sinners; and purify [your] hearts, [ye] double minded.** [Emp. added]   James 4:3-8

When we draw near to God by seeking Him with all our hearts, then He will draw near to us. The children of Israel were more interested in their own desires (lusts) than in God's. They were adulterers and adulteresses seeking the comfort and security the world's system could bring them. They soon forgot that all these luxuries and provisions couldn't save the Egyptians or their army. God says in order to draw near to Him, we must do two things.

First, we must cleanse our hands. II Corinthians 7:1 says,

"Having therefore these promises, dearly beloved, let us **cleanse ourselves** from all filthiness of the flesh and spirit, perfecting holiness in the fear of God" [Emp. added]. Sin separates us from God. Isaiah 59:2 says, "But your iniquities have **separated** between you and your God, and your sins have hid his face from you, that he will not hear" [Emp. added].

Second, we must purify our hearts. The key to this is what James said, "Purify your hearts, you **double minded**" [Emp. added]. The double-minded man is the man who fluctuates back and forth from the Spirit to the flesh. He has not **set** his mind on the things above. Colossians 3:1-2 says, "If ye then be risen with Christ, **seek** those things which are above, where Christ sitteth on the right hand of God. **Set** your affection on things above, not on things on the earth" [Emp. added].

What you are diligently **seeking** is that on which you will have your affections **set**. The key word is **set**. When a woman has her hair permed, each hair is chemically altered and set in curls. Now she no longer has straight hair; she has curly hair. It has been **set**. You can pull that hair straight, but when the tension is released it will bounce back to where it is **set**. A person can go to church, sing in the choir, and participate in Christian activities, but when he is not doing something "Christian," where is his mind? It will be where it is **set**. When he leaves the church or Christian atmosphere, his mind will bounce back to what it is **set** on, just as the permed hair does when the pressure is released from it. I've talked with many in churches around the country who sing in the meetings, agree with the messages, and give their time to work in the church. But in between the meetings, all they discuss is money, professional sports, clothes, the opposite sex, shopping experiences, and other things of the world. They "light up" when discussing those things, but going to church, reading the Bible, or praying is something they do out of obligation. Excitement is in their voice when they talk about their hobbies, but a monotone voice is heard when they talk about the things of God. Where is their mind **set**? Where is your mind **set**?

When a man falls in love with a woman and gets engaged to be married, you don't have to tell that man to think and talk about her all day. She's on his mind constantly. He talks about her to everyone who will listen. There is a spark in his voice as he speaks of her. The reason is that his affection, or heart, is **set** on her. His mind is not double. He is not thinking about other women. He is in love!

David said in Psalm 16:8, "I have **set** the LORD **always** before me: . . ." [Emp. added]. His mind was not double. His heart was pure. He did not have other things in his heart that he loved as he loved the Lord. **Things that we love, like, or trust in more than Jesus are called idols.**

Psalm 24:3-4 says: "Who may ascend into the hill of the Lord? Or who may stand in His holy place? He who has **clean hands** and **a pure heart, Who has not lifted up his soul to an idol,** Nor sworn deceitfully" [Emp. added]. The man who does not love, like, or trust in anything or person more than Jesus is the man who has a pure heart. There is one love in his heart, and that is the Lord. Jesus said in Matthew 10:37, "He that loveth father or mother more than me is not worthy of me: and he that loveth son or daughter more than me is not worthy of me."

In the time of the wilderness, let us draw near to God with clean hands and a pure heart as David, Moses, Paul, and other great men and women of God did. Let us not be as the children of Israel, who loved their lives and idols and missed their opportunity to know God.

Isaiah 35:1-2 says, ". . . **the desert** shall rejoice, and blossom as the rose. It shall blossom abundantly, and rejoice even with joy and singing: the glory of Lebanon shall be given unto it, the excellency of Carmel and Sharon, **they shall see the glory of the LORD, [and] the excellency of our God**" [Emp. added]. It is in the wilderness that the glory of the Lord is revealed!

CHAPTER 16

DRAWING FROM THE WELLS

*Many give up in these dry times,
but God is saying keep pressing
onward, don't stop!*

If anyone **thirsts**, let him come to Me and
drink. He who believes in Me, as the
Scripture has said, **out of his heart** will flow
rivers of living water. But this He spoke
concerning **the Spirit**, ... [Emp. added]
John 7:37-39 (NKJV)

The wilderness is a dry and thirsty land (Psalm 63:1).
Rain is scarce in the desert. Water is not accessed easily in
this place. In the wilderness, water must be drawn from
wells or springs that come from the earth. Jesus said that
rivers or springs of living water will flow out of the heart
of one who comes to Him and drinks. It is not the outpouring (rain) of the Spirit of God that we experience in the
desert, but water must be drawn from the wells of the
heart. In this dry place it is important that we draw the
water of refreshing from the fountain or well of God. Jesus
said to the woman at the well of Samaria, "Whosoever

drinketh of this water [natural water] shall thirst again: But whosoever drinketh of the water that I shall give him shall never thirst; but the water that I shall give him shall be in him a well of water springing up into everlasting life" [Emp. added] (John 4:13-14). Notice John 7:39 points out that He spoke of the well-source being the Spirit of the Lord, and that rivers (plural), not a river (singular), would flow from his heart.

The Spirit of the Lord manifests itself in several ways. Isaiah 11:2 shows some of His manifestations, "And the spirit of the LORD shall rest upon him, the spirit of wisdom and understanding, the spirit of counsel and might, the spirit of knowledge and of the fear of the LORD; ..."

He is called the Spirit of Wisdom, the Spirit of Understanding, the Spirit of Counsel, the Spirit of Might, the Spirit of Knowledge, and the Spirit of the Fear of the Lord.

Jesus said in regard to the Spirit of the Lord that He would manifest Himself as rivers of living water. So there would be a river of Wisdom, a river of Understanding, a river of Counsel, a river of Might, a river of Knowledge, and a river of the Fear of the Lord.

Proverb 18:4 says, "The words of a man's mouth are deep waters; the **wellspring** of **wisdom** is a flowing brook" [Emp. added]. Wisdom is one of the rivers.

Proverb 16:22 says, "**Understanding** is a **wellspring** of life to him who has it" [Emp. added]. Understanding is another river.

Proverb 20:5 says, "**Counsel** in the heart of man is like **deep water**, but a man of understanding will **draw** it out" [Emp. added]. Counsel is still another river.

These wells are resident in the heart of a Spirit-filled believer because this is where the Spirit abides. However, it is only the man who understands the ways of the Lord who will draw the waters out of the well. The key word in the above scripture is DRAW. The waters of refreshing in the wilderness do not come from the rain of the Spirit but must be *drawn* from the heart.

Proverb 10:11 says, "The **mouth** of the righteous is a **well of life**, . . ." [Emp. added].

Isaiah 12:3 says, "Therefore with joy you will draw water from the wells of salvation" [Emp. added].

I recall several instances when I would go out to pray in dry seasons and find it difficult. One such time I took my tent to a state park down the street from our house to spend the evening and next morning seeking the Lord. That night I prayed, then I read, then I began to sing songs of praise. I spent approximately three hours that evening doing these things, and it seemed I was getting nowhere. Nothing seemed fresh. I was as dry as could be. I finally went to bed and was very disappointed. That night it seemed to me as if the devils were having a celebration about me. The next morning I awoke unrefreshed. I began to walk the paths of the state park praying in the Spirit and still feeling very dry. This went on another hour and a half. I finally looked up and said, "Lord, I guess I am in the wilderness." My thoughts were, "I might as well go home and quit seeking Him; He has me in this dry place, and things won't change until He brings me out." This was erroneous thinking! God does not bring us into these times to frustrate us and get us to give up until He sovereignly takes us out! The wilderness is not intended to be a place of failure, but of victory! All of a sudden I heard a still small voice within say, "FIGHT." With that still small voice came a spark of fire and life.

Immediately I began to say, "Stir up the gift of God in me, Come forth rivers of living water, Spring up O well into my soul, Spring up O well and come forth rivers of God." Look what happened with Israel in the desert, "And from thence they went to Beer: that is the well whereof the LORD spake unto Moses, Gather the people together, and I will give them water. Then Israel sang this song, **Spring up, O well**; sing ye unto it: . . ." [Emp. added] (Numbers 21:16-17).

As I kept repeating these words, the prayer became more and more intense until I found myself pacing up and down that path, praying and speaking the Word of the Lord

with great strength and fire. Everything was fresh, and I
was like a different person. His presence was manifested in
a strong way. Just minutes earlier I had felt heavy and
weak, but now I was ready to face any enemy with the
Word of the Lord. This lasted about twenty-five minutes,
but it seemed like only five. I was refreshed totally and
ready to go forth.

Proverb 15:23 says, "A man has **joy** by the answer of his
mouth" [Emp. added]. If I had walked away from that
campsite saying, "I might as well go home and quit seeking
Him, He has me in this dry place, and things won't change
until He brings me out," it would have kept me in the state
of heaviness I was fighting. But because I spoke what God
put into my heart, it gave me the joy I needed to draw from
the wells. I had tapped into the wells of salvation and was
drawing out the water of refreshing. It was like drinking
cool water from a spring in the middle of the desert!

Many give up in these dry times, but God is saying, "Keep
pressing onward; don't stop!" We must have a persistent and
tenacious drive within us that won't let us stop until His will
is done. Many stop praying when they feel dry; they stop
because no water is coming from the wells, and it seems too
difficult to obtain. They are weak, and God wants their
strength built up for battles they will face in the future. Just
because you don't feel His presence in the prayer closet does
not mean He is denying you. **He is drawing you!**

UNSTOPPING THE WELLS

In Genesis 26:1-18, we find Isaac in a place of dryness.
Verses 1-3 say, "And there was a **famine** in the land, beside
the first famine that was in the days of Abraham. . . . And
the LORD appeared unto him, and said, Go **not** down into
Egypt; dwell in the land which I shall tell thee of: Sojourn in
this land, and **I will be with thee, and will bless thee;** . . ."
[Emp. added].

God specifically tells Isaac not to run to Egypt where it is comfortable, but to stay in the land to which He had led him. Many times when we find ourselves in a dry place, the first thing that comes to mind is, "I'm getting out of here!" If it is dry in the prayer closet, we will think of all the things we need to do in our day and leave the prayer closet. If it seems dry to us in the church we attend, the thought comes, "I'm going to where there is a move of God." Or if it seems dry in our social or business life, the thought comes of leaving and finding a city with economic prosperity. We think, "If I stay here, I'll dry up and never see the plan of God fulfilled in my life." There are so many Christians who do just that in America. They run from activity to activity, from church to church, from city to city trying to find a church or city that is not "dry." Instead of digging the wells and allowing God to use them to bring refreshing to that dry place, they go seeking the place of ease! What they don't understand is that in many of these instances God intends to bring forth the vision He has given them right there in that "dry place." I am not saying this is always the case. There are times when God prepares us for a new place and allows the old to dry up. Be led by the Spirit of God! If He is not saying anything, then stay and fight!

Look at what happens to Isaac as a result of obeying God and staying in that land of famine.

> Then Isaac sowed in that land, and received in the same year an hundredfold: and the LORD blessed him. And the man waxed great, and went forward, and grew until he became very great: For he had possession of flocks, and possession of herds, and great store of servants: and the Philistines envied him. **For all the wells** which his father's servants had digged in the days of Abraham his father, **the Philistines had stopped them, and filled**

> **them with earth. . . . And Isaac digged again**
> **the wells of water,** which they had digged
> in the days of Abraham his father; for the
> Philistines had stopped them after the death
> of Abraham; and he called their names after
> the names by which his father had called
> them. [Emp. added]   Genesis 26:12-15, 18

The water he needed for his crops to grow was obtained
by redigging the wells that his father had once dug. These
wells were plugged up by the Philistines. Over a period of
time, the enemy had stopped up the wells. Just as with
Isaac, the water we so desperately need for the growth of
God's incorruptible seed to mature in our hearts must be
drawn from stopped-up wells.

The worldliness presently in the Church (the Body of
Christ) has stopped many wells. A Church that once was
very fruitful now has become dry because it has allowed
the enemy to seduce it. God is in the process of restoring us
back to where we once were. This applies to us both personally and to the Church as a whole in America. Isaiah
58:11-13 says:

> And the LORD shall guide thee continu-
> ally, and satisfy thy soul in **drought,** and
> make fat thy bones: and thou shalt be like a
> **watered garden,** and like **a spring of water,**
> **whose waters fail not.** And they that shall
> be of thee shall **build the old waste places:**
> thou shalt **raise up the foundations of many**
> **generations;** and thou shalt be called, The
> **repairer of the breach, The restorer of paths**
> **to dwell in.** If thou . . . shalt honour him [the
> Lord by], **not doing thine own ways, nor**
> **finding thine own pleasure, nor speaking**
> **thine own words:** . . . [Emp. added]

As Isaac did not seek his own way or pleasure by going to the land of ease, so we (if we will not do things our way, or seek our own pleasure, nor speak our own words, but honor God) shall be like a watered garden and a spring of living water whose waters do not fail! God will bring his living water to dry and thirsty places through these people.

God is leading us to redig those wells that the world has plugged up. Again, that takes persistence. It may take longer than an hour to reopen a well; it may take longer than two hours; it may take longer than a day; it may take longer than a week! You say, "How long will it take?" The answer is, "It shouldn't matter to you; just keep digging until you tap it." There will be many times when it is not done in one session of prayer—you will have to pick up again the next time you come into your prayer closet. A very dear friend of mine and I used to pray together nearly every morning when I lived in Dallas, Texas. He was one of several pastors in the church, and I was an assistant to the head pastor and his wife. We would come into that room at 7:00 a.m. We would pray in the Spirit and could sense the progress, but there were many times when 8:30 a.m. would arrive (which was when work started) and we would have to leave and go to work. We would almost feel frustrated because there was absolutely no breakthrough . . . no waters of refreshing. The next morning we would come in and pick up almost exactly where we left off. This would go on sometimes for two days, other times three days, and one particular time I remember it taking a week! However, when the breakthrough came—wow! What power and refreshing.

As I travel to churches across America, I can spot the many Christians who have allowed their wells to be plugged up and have settled comfortably into that state. The alarming fact is that it is the majority—not the minority—that is in this condition. What would happen if these people stirred up the gift in them and allowed it to be released? Homes would be changed; churches would be changed—America would be changed! The gift of God is lying dormant in our homes, our churches, and our nation. The wells are plugged while Christians boast of being "Spirit-filled."

The Church will not be revived until we as individuals are revived! The Church is not an organization; it is the people of God, and the condition of God's people is the condition of the Church!

CHAPTER 17

VICTORY IN THE WILDERNESS

. . . prophetic vision is to see the way God sees . . .

> Where there is no revelation [**prophetic vision**], the people **cast off restraint**; . . .
> [Emp. added]   Proverbs 29:18

The prophetic vision is to see things the way God sees them. It is to discern the purpose of heaven in a time or season of our life, as well as to perceive the destination God has set before us when it still is not manifest to the natural eye, and even seems as if it will never happen.

Our focus must be on the purpose of God, not on the resistance we face that tries to keep us from pressing on to the destination set before us. We must have the right vision before us if we are to finish at the right destination! It would be a terrible thing to run a race and cross the wrong finish line! It would be a disaster to aim at the wrong target and hit it! The Pharisees were very zealous and diligent, but their purpose was self-seeking; they did not have the prophetic vision; therefore, they were missing the mark.

157

What is the destination and purpose of God for us as a Church and for you as a member of the Church, His body? In Ephesians 1:11, He says that we have been "... **predestined** according to the **purpose** of Him who works all things according to the counsel of His will" [Emp. added]. Predestination is a word over which many have stumbled. In order to understand it, we must break apart the word and look at it by the root and prefix. The prefix "pre" simply means "before" or "prior to the beginning." The root "destination" means "where you will end" or "the finish line." Putting the two together, it means "to set the finish line before the start." Ephesians 1:11, therefore, shows us that God set a **destination** for mankind—prior to creating us—that would fulfill His **purpose**.

Romans 8:28-29 says, "And we know that all things work together for good to those who love God, to those who are the called according to **His purpose**. For whom He foreknew, He also **predestined** to be **conformed** to the **image of His Son**, that He might be the firstborn among many brethren" [Emp. added].

Our **destination**, which God planned before time began, was for us who love God to be conformed to the image of Jesus Christ. Everything done in life or ministry should be toward this goal or end! God's purpose for creating you was not just so you could cast out devils, or heal the sick, or win the lost to Jesus. There have been many who have done those things but never crossed the finish line. The reason is that their focus was on the ministry and not the goal or heart behind the ministry!

Now the question must be answered, "What was the **purpose** of God in predestining us to be conformed to the image of Jesus Christ?" The answer is simple—because He loved us and desired fellowship with us so "that in the ages to come He might show the exceeding riches of His grace in His kindness toward us in Christ Jesus" [Emp. added] (Ephesians 2:7, NKJV).

That was His purpose right from the beginning. When

He created man and placed him in the garden, the Lord walked and had fellowship with Adam because of His love for him. One of Adam's descendants caught hold of the purpose of God, and it is recorded of him that, "**Enoch walked with God**; and he was not, for God took him" [Emp. added] (Genesis 5:24). The writer of Hebrews says that "... he had this testimony, that **he pleased God**" [Emp. added] (Hebrews 11:5). Why did Enoch please God? Was it because he had a great prophetic ministry? Or because he had a great evangelistic ministry? No and No again! It was because **HE WALKED WITH GOD!** He had fellowship with God.

Everything that God has done in the past, is doing now, and will be doing in the future in regard to the Church will be for that purpose. So the purpose of the wilderness is to point us in the direction of being conformed to the image of Jesus Christ.

If we lose sight of the purpose of God in our lives, we will cast off restraint and begin to backslide. As a Church, if we lose sight of the purpose of God, we will cast off restraint and begin to dry up. Then the thrust will be to get results and grow in numbers, rather than making disciples in the image of Jesus Christ (Matthew 28:19).

Let's look again at Proverb 29:18: "Where there is no revelation [**prophetic vision**], the people **cast off restraint;** ..." [Emp. added]. Of what restraint is God speaking? It is the restraint that keeps us from settling for the low call, which is anything short of being conformed to His image and likeness. It is the restraint that keeps us from being satisfied until we behold Him face to face and see His glory revealed. It is the restraint that keeps us from accepting anything short of His perfect will. This restraint will keep us from being at ease and doing things the way the world does them. It will keep us from doing things the way of the flesh.

In speaking of **vision**, Jesus said, "The lamp of the body is the eye. If therefore your eye is good, your whole body will be full of light. But if your eye is bad, your whole body

will be full of darkness" (Matthew 6:22-23, NKJV). To
understand what He is saying, we must realize that He is
not speaking of the physical eye. He is speaking of the eye
of the heart, or the way you **perceive** things.

The way you **perceive** things in your heart is the way
you will become. Proverb 23:7 says, "For as he thinks in his
heart, so is he."

The way you **perceive** the circumstances in which you
find yourself or the situations that you are facing will determine how you come through them.

The twelve leaders of the children of Israel who went to
spy out the promised land all saw the same sights. They all
saw the same fortified cities, the same giants, and the same
armies of the Canaanite nations. However, two of them **saw**
it in a totally different way than the other ten. Two **perceived** it the way God saw it, and the ten **perceived** it
through the eyes of natural experience or through the eyes
of their own ability. Because their **eyes** were bad, the rest of
their behavior (or as Jesus said, "their whole body") was
the same. They spoke with their mouths and responded
with their actions in a manner contrary to the will of God.
God said their report was "evil" or "bad."

Numbers 14:28-30 shows the results of their wrong perception. God said:

> Say unto them, [As truly as] I live, saith
> the LORD, **as ye have spoken in mine ears,
> so will I do to you:** Your carcases shall fall in
> this wilderness; and all that were numbered
> of you, according to your whole number,
> from twenty years old and upward, which
> have murmured against me, Doubtless **ye
> shall not come into the land, concerning
> which I sware to make you dwell therein,**
> except Caleb the son of Jephunneh, and
> Joshua the son of Nun. [Emp. added]
> Numbers 14:28-30

What caused them to speak in His ears that which would cause them never to see what He had promised them? It was how they **perceived** what was before them. They did not have the prophetic vision; they had their own vision. What they saw was what they spoke. They saw it not through God's eyes, but through their own limited natural ability.

In order to come through the wilderness victoriously, we must **see** things the way God **sees** them. The children of Israel already had been complaining for more than a year before God sent the spies into the promised land. Their **vision** was already bad, and all restraint was cast off, so that by the time God allowed them to see the land that flowed with milk and honey, they rejected it.

Those who see only the wilderness (and the hardships associated with it) will die in their wilderness. Those who keep their eyes set on the Promiser and vision He has set before them will come through the wilderness as sanctified warriors, ready to take the promised land set before them to the glory of God.

> Therefore we do not lose heart [faint or cast off restraint]; . . . For our **light affliction, which is but for a moment,** is **working** for us a **far more exceeding and eternal weight of glory,** while we do not **look** at the things which are **seen,** but at the things which are **not seen** [perceiving things the way God does]. For the things which are **seen are temporary** [subject to change], but the things which are **not seen are eternal.** [Emp. added]   II Corinthinans 4:16-18 (NKJV)

The sufferings experienced in the wilderness, compared with its yield, are considered **light.** The length of time spent in the wilderness, compared with its yield, is considered a **moment.** Now, when you are in the middle of it, that seems hard to believe unless you have the **vision of what is**

beyond it. When I was in the middle of the dry times in my
past, they sure didn't seem like a "moment" at the time.
Sometimes I thought, "Is this going to end? Is what God
promised ever going to come to pass?" That is when I
quickly had to cast down those thoughts and encourage
myself in the Lord. I would remember the prophecies previously made concerning me, and by them wage a good
warfare (I Timothy 1:18). The prophecies were the vision of
God for my life as He revealed it to me by His Spirit through
His Word.

II Peter 2:11 says, "Beloved, I beg you as sojourners and
pilgrims, abstain from fleshly lusts [desires] which **war**
against the **soul, . . .**" [Emp. added]. The soul is the **battlefield** in the wilderness. The soul consists of your intellect,
emotions, and will. The *will* is that part of your soul which
decides whether you will go God's way or the way of
flesh—if you will **see** things as God does or if you will give
attention to your affliction in the wilderness.

It all comes down to **"WHO IS THE CENTER OF
FOCUS?"** You or the Lord? The fleshly desires that war in
your intellect and emotions will focus on selfish interests.
These will draw you away from the "prophetic vison," for
God's way is not the way of self, but the way of *denying* self.

The gospel that has been preached and accepted by
many in these latter days has been a gospel of ease. The
focus has been "What can God do for me?" rather than
"What does He desire of me?" The gospel of ease has not
spoken of the sufferings involved in pursuing Christ.
Rather, it has been a gospel that has appealed to the desires
of the flesh. It has caused many to settle down into a complacent life-style. It has not equipped believers to be the soldiers God has called us to be. II Timothy 2:3-4 says, "Thou
therefore **endure hardness, as a good soldier of Jesus
Christ.** No man that **warreth** entangleth himself with the
affairs of this life; that he may please him who hath chosen
him to be a **soldier**" [Emp. added]. Because of this "gospel
of ease," if resistance or hardship comes in the course of our

lives, we seek an escape route, rather than pressing on through it. The vision that is birthed by this kind of teaching is not the **"heavenly or prophetic vision,"** but rather a **"selfish vision."**

Paul said in Acts 26:19-21, "Whereupon, O king Agrippa, I was not disobedient unto the **heavenly vision:** But shewed first unto them of Damascus, and at Jerusalem, and throughout all the coasts of Judaea, and then to the Gentiles, that they should repent and turn to God, and do works meet for repentance. For **these causes the Jews caught me in the temple, and went about to kill me"** [Emp. added].

There are many visions in the world, but only one "heavenly vision." Heaven has only one vision and that is the will of the Father!

Notice Paul said, "For these reasons the Jews seized me in the temple and tried to kill me." He was pursuing the heavenly vision and experiencing great **resistance** to it. If he believed the gospel of ease, as many have preached and believed today, he never would have seen the vision fulfilled. He would not even have made it to Agrippa, because much earlier he would have sought the way of escape from the resistance experienced as a result of journeying toward the vision God set before him.

Jeremiah was a man who was pursuing the heavenly vision and experiencing a lot of verbal and mental persecution as a result of his obedience. He became weary of it one day and began to complain a little. He said, ". . . Why does the way of the wicked prosper? Why are those happy who deal so treacherously?" (Jeremiah 12:1, NKJV). God did not come back to him with a sympathetic answer. **Sympathy is an enemy that will cause you to focus on yourself.** God said to him, "If you have run with the footmen, and they have wearied you, Then how can you contend with horses? . . ." (Jeremiah 12:5, NKJV). In other words, God was saying, "Jeremiah, if you are getting weary of the devil's foot soldiers, what are you going to do when you face the devil's cavalry?" To put it even more plainly, God was saying, "If you are weary and think it is bad now, you haven't seen anything yet! Prepare yourself, because the resistance you have been facing is going to get worse!" (paraphrased).

We must remember that there are no great victories where there are no great battles. It did get tougher for Jeremiah. He went from being verbally abused to being thrown into prison, and still later he was thrown into a dungeon and left to die. However, God delivered him from all of the afflictions and persecutions that he faced.

The battles that most in the body of Christ are experiencing today are mental attacks, not the physical persecution that Paul experienced. What will we do when the resistance gets worse? The afflictions we endure presently will strengthen us to handle greater battles in the future.

The wilderness is boot camp and training ground for future battles. Just as we send soldiers to boot camp to prepare them for war, even so God sends His enlisted soldiers to the wilderness to prepare them for the ministry to which He has called them. The greatest obstacle soldiers have to overcome in boot camp is themselves. Likewise, the greatest battle one experiences in the wilderness is in the realm of the soul.

The war experienced in the wilderness is the battle that rages in the soul. The enemy's purpose is to get your focus on you. That is what he tried to do with Jesus in the wilderness. Jesus was hungry from not eating for forty days and the devil came and said, "If You are the Son of God, command that these stones become bread" (Matthew 4:1-11). The temptation was to use the power of God apart from God's way to provide what His flesh needed. We must remember that when God gives a gift, it comes with an awesome responsibility not to misuse it, but to administer it as He desires. God was going to minister to the needs of Jesus, but it would be done His way. For after the devil left, the angels came and ministered to Jesus.

Again, let's look at what Jesus said concerning His ministry: "Verily, verily, I say unto you, The Son can do nothing of himself, but what he **seeth** the Father do: for what things soever he doeth, these also doeth the Son likewise" [Emp. added] (John 5:19). Notice the word **seeth**. He did nothing apart from the **prophetic vision**.

When in dry times, one of our temptations will be to do it our own way, rather than waiting on God's way. This could entail using God's power to get something before His time. Can you imagine a soldier in a battle not fighting according to his superior officer's orders, but doing it his own way? This could result in serious damage to the soldier and those around him. In boot camp that soldier learns to obey, so that he will not foolishly risk losing his life and the lives of those around him in intense battle. He will obey the command of his leader.

It is important that we keep before us what heaven has revealed to us. There will be times when we think, "I have got to have an answer NOW!" or "I have got to make a move now; if I do nothing, everything will fall apart!" If God is not saying anything, that means He is speaking. He is saying, "You don't need to do anything now." In those situations we must WAIT on the Lord. Don't force it! "Wait on the LORD: be of good courage, and he shall strengthen thine heart: wait, I say, on the LORD" (Psalm 27:14).

If we focus on our needs and not on Him, discouragement and heaviness will set in. We cannot look at the "light affliction," but we must keep our eyes on the "exceeding and eternal weight of glory that is being worked for us in the affliction." This is the joy set before us on which we must keep our eyes.

THE JOY SET BEFORE US

My brethren, count it **all joy** when ye fall
into divers temptations; Knowing [this], that
the trying of your faith **worketh** patience

[endurance]. But let patience [endurance]
have [her] perfect work, that ye may be perfect [mature] and entire, wanting nothing.
[Emp. added]   James 1:2-4

Notice God says, "Count it ALL joy!" Notice He does not
say, "Count it part joy and part sorrow." There is not to be any
admixture of sorrow in our hearts. Now, it is easy to "count it
all joy" when everything is going great. But that is not what
He says. The time to "count it all joy" is in the time of trials.
Why does God say this? Because He knows that ". . . **the joy
of the LORD is your strength**" [Emp. added] (Nehemiah
8:10). Joy is a spiritual force that gives us strength to endure
afflictions and trials.

What is the joy of the Lord? For years I thought that the
joy of the Lord was to have the joy that He has. I had a hard
time relating to that. However, that is not what He is saying. Have you ever heard someone make a statement like,
"The joy of cooking"? Cooking has no joy in itself. What
they are saying is that you will experience joy in cooking.
The "joy of the Lord" is the joy we experience from our relationship with Him. HE BRINGS US JOY!

My wife and three boys bring me joy! There are times
when I am away from home that looking at a picture of them
brings joy to my heart. It brings strength to me. That is what
Nehemiah was saying to the men. They were going through a
tough time. There was a lot of resistance coming against them,
so Nehemiah cried out, "Don't sorrow over this persecution—
get your eyes on the Lord. Because when you look at the Lord,
joy will fill your heart and it will be strength to you."

Praise will cause your focus to turn from you to the
Lord. In the midst of trials, it is easy to lose sight of the ability of God because of the intense pressure of the resistance
you face. David wrote most of the book of Psalms, and the
majority of his Psalms was written in the middle of trials.
By praising God, he was able to stay strong in the midst of
adverse circumstances.

In Isaiah 61:3, God says that He gives us "the oil of **joy** for mourning and the **garment of praise** for the spirit of **heaviness;** . . ." [Emp. added].

One day during a dry time while I was at home alone, heaviness set in. I picked up my Bible to read and could barely do it. So I began to pray and that was even worse. Inside I could sense that the Spirit of God was saying to me, "Turn on one of your praise tapes." So I went up to our loft where our stereo system is located and turned on some praise music and began to sing along with it. When the medley of songs was over, I felt impressed to play them again. The second time through, I began to hear what I was singing. Joy began to spring up into my soul, and I began to dance and sing all over that loft. I noticed that my eyes had gotten off of myself and on the greatness of Jesus. For the next thirty minutes I was dancing and singing. The heaviness was gone totally, and I had life and strength flowing out of me where there had been none just thirty minutes earlier.

Isaiah 12:3 says, "Therefore with **joy** shall ye **draw water** out of the wells of **salvation**" [Emp. added]. As I was praising Him my focus was turned back toward Him, and through the joy of the Lord I began to draw strength from the wells of salvation.

Praise will help keep our eyes on the joy set before us, rather than on the circumstances that surround us.

> Wherefore seeing we also are compassed about with so great a cloud of witnesses, let us lay aside every weight, and the sin which doth so easily beset [us], and **let us run with patience [endurance] the race that is set before us,** Looking unto Jesus the **author** and **finisher** of [our] faith; **who for the *joy* that was set before him endured the cross,** despising the shame, and is set down at the right hand of the throne of God. For consid-

er him that endured such contradiction of
sinners against himself, lest ye be **wearied
and faint in your minds.** Ye have not yet
resisted unto blood, striving against sin.
[Emp. added]   Hebrews 12:1-4

Jesus endured the greatest trial that anyone ever *has*
faced or ever *will* face, by keeping His eyes on the JOY set
before Him. The joy set before Him was the resurrection
that followed the crucifixion. It was the glory that would
follow the obedience of suffering. This would bring many
sons and daughters into His kingdom.

That is the way it is for us who follow in His steps. Beyond
denying self and crucifying the flesh awaits RESURREC-
TION LIFE. Beyond the sufferings of the flesh is the glory of
God! "For I consider that the **sufferings of this present time**
are not worthy to be compared with the **glory** which shall be
revealed in us" [Emp. added] (Romans 8:18).

God's glory will be revealed in the Church prior to His
return. The magnitude of it will be so great that it will draw
cities and nations to His salvation. Never before has the
earth seen such a demonstration of His power as will be
manifested in the ones who have allowed God to purify
them. This revival, which will lead into the great harvest,
will need no promotion by man. It will be promoted by His
power and glory!

Beloved, do not think it strange concerning the **fiery trial** which is to try you, as
though some strange thing happened to
you; but **rejoice** to the **extent** that you par-
take of **Christ's sufferings,** that when **His
glory is revealed,** you may also be glad with
exceeding joy. [Emp. added] I Peter 4:12-13

What is the joy set before us? It is His glory being revealed
in us who have suffered as a result of obedience to Christ!

Notice that the extent to which you suffer is the extent to which you should rejoice, knowing that the greater the resistance, the greater the glory! Keep your eyes on the joy set before us, which is His glory manifested in us. This will give you the strength to overcome the trials you face.

A FINAL WORD

I want to exhort you to continue to press on "Until the spirit be poured upon us from on high, and the wilderness be a fruitful field, and the fruitful field be counted for a forest" (Isaiah 32:15).

The wilderness is **not** the place where we are to lay down our weapons of war and give up! It is the place where we are to be strong, bold, and courageous to do the will of the Lord. It is the place we are to submit ourselves to God and resist the devil steadfastly. But remember, we must discern between what is the devil and what is flesh! You cannot "cast out" flesh—you must deal with it through repentance. God has brought you into this place so that *you* may know what is in your heart. What many times I initially thought was the devil were really areas of my life that needed to be submitted to Christ but had been hidden to me.

As you continue your pursuit of the high call of God in Christ, remember these words of exhortation: II Corinthians 2:14 says, "Now thanks [be] unto God, which **always** causeth us to **triumph in Christ** . . ." [Emp. added].

Romans 8:35,37 says, "Who shall separate us from the love of Christ? shall tribulation, or distress, or persecution, or famine, or nakedness, or peril, or sword? Nay, in all these things we are **more than conquerors through Him** that loved us" [Emp. added].

I Corinthians 15:57 says, "But thanks [be] to God, which **giveth us the victory** through our Lord Jesus Christ" [Emp. added].

Do not quit your pursuit of Him. Do not give up. Keep the

vision before you, no matter how the circumstances appear.

It seemed hopeless for Joseph in the pit, but when he was thrown into the dungeon it appeared to be over. Now it seemed impossible for the vision ever to come to pass. Remember, "With men it is impossible, but not with God: for **with God all things are possible**" [Emp. added] (Mark 10:27).

Even so with you—no matter how tough it gets, remember that ". . . all things are possible to him that believeth" (Mark 9:23). Continue to seek Him with all your heart, and believe what He speaks to you by His Spirit through His Word, that you may experience "VICTORY IN THE WILDERNESS!"

May God's high call be yours in Christ Jesus!

ON THE AUTHOR

JOHN P. BEVERE, JR.

John Bevere attended Purdue University, graduating in 1981 with a Bachelor of Science degree in Mechanical Engineering. While at Purdue, John played varsity tennis and was a member of a fraternity. It was while in this fraternity that John was born again in January 1979 and filled with the Spirit on June 3 of that same year.

John attended Word of Faith Bible and Leadership institute in Dallas, Texas, in 1981 and 1982. He then worked as Executive Staff Assistant at Word of Faith World Outreach Center, from June 1983 through November 1987.

From November 1987 to December 1989, John was the Youth/College/Career Pastor at Orlando Christian Center under Benny Hinn. In January 1990, John resigned from staff to travel fulltime. Presently John travels from coast to coast and border to border, preaching the message God has put in his heart. John's vision for this nation is to see revival and restoration come through the prophetic preaching of repentance, prayer, holiness, and spiritual warfare . . . joining arms with local pastors to pull down strongholds and turn the hearts of the people back to God.

John and his wife, Lisa, reside in the Orlando, Florida area and have three young sons—Addison David, Austin Michael, and Joshua Alexander.

OTHER BOOKS BY
John Bevere

1) THE VOICE OF ONE CRYING

God is restoring the prophetic to turn the heart of His people to Him. Yet often this office is reduced to merely one who predicts the future by a word of knowledge or wisdom . . . rather than a declaration of the church's true condition and destiny. Many, fed up with hype and superficial ministry, are ready to receive the true prophetic message.

SOME ISSUES ADDRESSED IN THIS BOOK:

- Genuine vs. counterfeit conversion
- Message of the true prophetic
- Recognizing false prophets
- The Elijah anointing
- Idolatry in America
- Exposing deception

2) THE BAIT OF SATAN

This book exposes one of the most deceptive snares Satan uses to get believers out of the will of God. It is the trap of offense.

Most who are ensnared do not even realize it. But everyone must be made aware of this trap, because Jesus said, "It is impossible that offenses will not come" (Luke 17:1). The question is not, Will you encounter the bait of Satan? Rather it is, How will you respond? Your response determines your future! Don't let another person's sin or mistake affect your relationship with God!

"This book by my friend John Bevere is strong, strong, strong! I found new help from his fresh insights and uncompromising desire to help each of us recognize Satan's baits and avoid them at all costs."

Oral Roberts
Oral Roberts University

3) BREAKING INTIMIDATION
How to Overcome Fear and
Release the Gift of God in Your Life

Countless Christians battle intimidation. Yet they wrestle with the side effects rather than the source. Intimidation is rooted in the fear of man. Proverbs 29:25 says, "The fear of man brings a snare . . . " This snare limits us so we don't reach our full potential.

Paul admonished Timothy, "The gift of God in you is dormant because you're intimidated!" (2 Tim. 1:6-7, paraphrased). An intimidated believer loses his position of spiritual authority. Without this authority his gifting from God remains dormant.

The bible is filled with examples of God's people facing intimidation. Some overcame while others were overcome. This book is an in-depth look at these ancient references and present day scenarios. The goal: to expose intimidation, break it's fearful grip, and release God's gift and dominion in your life.

This is an urgent message for every child of God who desires to reach their full potential in their walk with Christ. Don't allow fear to hold you back.

VIDEO CASSETTE MESSAGES
by John Bevere

$15.00 each

Baptism of Fire   *The Bait of Satan*
Pursuing God   *Does God Know You?*
The Coming Glory   *Armed to Suffer*

AUDIO CASSETTE MESSAGES
by John Bevere

3 tape series ($15.00 each)   **2 tape series ($10.00 each)**
Walking with God   *Overcoming Offenses*
Pursue the High Call   *Joy in the Holy Ghost*
Breaking through Resistance   *Fresh Vision*
Birthing in the Spirit   *The Double Portion Anointing*
The Wilderness
Armed to Suffer

Postage and Handling: Orders to $15.00 . . . . . .$2.00
(For retail purchases) $15.01 to $30.00 . . . . . .$3.50
                           $30.01 to $50.00 . . . . . .$4.50
                           $50.00 and above $5.00

Bookstore and volume discounts available

To receive our free newsletter and a complete list of available materials from John Bevere Ministries, or for information on having John Bevere or his wife, Lisa, minister to your church, conference, retreat, or any other ministry group, please contact the ministry at the following address:

John Bevere Ministries
P.O. Box 2002
Apopka, Florida 32704-2002
(407) 889-9617

Feel free to include testimonies of how the Lord has ministered to you through this book or our other ministry materials.